Phyllis Sisson rolled into our church family one Sunday on a mission from God, unbeknownst to her, to bless and amaze. We were blessed by her great desire to serve the Lord despite being confined to a wheelchair and were amazed when the Lord chose to display His healing power in restoring her health. That special touch from the Lord would bolster her faith in the days to come when she was tested by trials.

—Rev. Bob MacGregor
Lead Pastor, Grandview

A True Story of Incredible Healing

MIRACLE
ON WORCHESTER AVENUE

PJ Sisson

MIRACLE ON WORCHESTER AVENUE
Copyright © 2024 by PJ Sisson

ISBN: 978-1-4866-2590-1
eBook ISBN: 978-1-4866-2591-8

Word Alive Press
119 De Baets Street Winnipeg, MB R2J 3R9
www.wordalivepress.ca

WORD ALIVE
—PRESS—

Cataloguing in Publication information can be obtained from Library and Archives Canada.

*This autobiography is dedicated to my siblings and our families,
in honour of our parents and to the glory of God!*

Contents

Acknowledgements

I thank my daughter Donna-Lee Sisson, who directed me to Word Alive Press; to my daughter and granddaughter Debra-Kaye and Caitlin Joice, for their technical assistance; and to my sons Dwight and Dean, who have supported me in whatever endeavour I embark upon. Thanks go to Janelle Rutledge and Maysee McLean for photography, and to the family members and friends who have encouraged me over the years to write this story. Thanks go to God for enabling me with the strength, memory, and time to write. May you, the reader, be encouraged to press on, no matter the circumstances in your life.

INTRODUCTION
A Miracle

My cousin Jean was shocked while attending our Uncle Elvin's funeral in 1999. This time, though, the shock was a pleasant one.

For twenty years after Dad passed away in 1979, Uncle Elvin had been like a father to me. It was very comforting to spend time with extended family and friends for a celebration of his life.

Uncle Elvin had been the youngest brother to both mine and Jean's fathers. She and I hadn't seen each other for several years and she was pleasantly surprised to see me walking again.

Jean was raised with two younger brothers and thought of me as a little sister. As we reminisced at the funeral, she shared how shocked she had been as a young schoolgirl to learn of my life-threatening polio diagnosis when I was taken to Toronto Sick Kids hospital. She knew it had been a lonely place for me at the age of four, being so many miles away from home and family. How she had wished to be with me!

In fact, the news had shaken her so much that she hadn't been able to bring herself to attend school that day. Jean had understood that many young Canadian children had died during what became known as the epidemic of '49 and had feared we may never see each other again.

After several months of recovery, our families continued to visit periodically until, as adults, Jean and I went our separate ways, living many miles apart. Jean knew of the challenges I faced of pain and weakness while living with the residual effects of polio.

She also spoke of how shocked she had been again in 1988 with the news that I could no longer walk at the age of forty-three. She'd heard that an electric wheelchair was my constant companion. Her heart had gone out to me, thinking, "What's next?"

Now she had the delightful shock of discovering that I could walk again. Jean was eager to hear the details. After hearing about the miracle, she replied, "Now you're as healthy as a horse." I can still hear her big hearty laugh and feel her tight bearhug, for which she was well known.

While updating each other, she was sad to hear of my husband's death, though, and then happy to hear of my remarriage and pleased that I was spending my time in religious work.

Merriam-Webster defines miracle in three ways:

- an extraordinary event manifesting divine intervention in human affairs.
- an extremely outstanding or unusual event, thing, or accomplishment.
- a divinely natural phenomenon experienced humanly as the fulfillment of spiritual law.[1]

The miracle on Worchester Avenue happened in 1995. It surely did bring welcome consequences.

I had been a full-time power wheelchair driver for seven years, having been given a comprehensive medical assessment telling me that I would remain as such.

Then, instantly, I became a healthy walking person.

My family doctor declared the happening to be a miracle. He then called in another colleague who asked five pertinent questions. Upon hearing the answers, he turned to my doctor and said, "We can't touch this. We have a miracle on our hands."

In the following weeks, a newspaper reporter searched to verify my disability and thereby lend further credence to the miracle. In his research, he contacted my previous doctor from the 1980s.

---

[1] "Miracle," Merriam-Webster. Date of access: July 25, 2024 (https://www.merriam-webster.com/dictionary/miracle).

"This must be another Phyllis Sisson," the doctor declared. "The Phyllis Sisson who was my patient in the 80s will never walk again."

There is no cure for a person living with the late effects of polio, also known as post-polio syndrome. It is a fact that such a person will take the pain, weakness, and disability to their grave.

However, at the time of this writing, I have been walking for the past twenty-nine years. I've also had the privilege to travel to twenty-three countries with a ministry of encouragement. This contradicts known scientific law and is hence thought to be due to supernatural causes, especially an act of God.

I give God the glory, as He fulfilled the desires of my heart to know Him, enjoy effective prayer, impact others, and experience the people and beauty of so many countries around the world.

Never once did I ask for a miracle. I knew, however, that God's grace was sufficient to spend the rest of my life in a wheelchair. Throughout my physical struggles, God had shown His faithfulness through people, the words of wisdom and love found in the Bible, the prayers of others, and nature. God is the giver of every natural breath and I trusted Him with my life, in whatever condition I found myself. If God chose to heal me, that would be great; if He chose not to heal me, His grace would continue to be sufficient.

On the day of the miracle—February 20, 1995—God spoke to me. I had heard His voice on two other occasions. Once when I was very ill and being transferred to Toronto General Hospital from our Minden Red Cross Hospital. The other was when my dad was dying. God spoke each time with a gentle, comforting, wise, loving, and authoritative voice.

On that February evening, on Worchester Avenue, I heard God say, *"Would you be willing to share with others what I am doing in your life?"*

That could have been a thought-provoking and time-consuming question. What did He mean? Did He mean the past, the present, or the future? Instead of pondering this, however, I answered in a split-second with a resounding yes. "Yes, God, I will share with others what You are doing in my life!"

This miracle was an obvious, life-changing event. I stood tall, 5'5", my back straight and strong. I remained standing without falling or fainting. All pain had been removed from my body. All weakness, gone. I no longer felt the discomfort that had been with me for forty-six years. There was no more shallow breathing. A muscle had appeared in my leg that had never developed properly. My deformed polio foot was transformed and lengthened. I had a feeling of complete wellness. It was amazing!

God had fixed my fifty-year-old body in the blink of an eye, or quicker. I felt well for the first time I could remember. God had changed my status from a disabled woman to a healthy one and He was saying, "Would You be willing to share with others what I am doing in your life?"

I knew I could trust Him with this restored body. I knew this awesome God! He was my heavenly Father! I knew I could say yes.

What I didn't know, and was about to discover, was that God doesn't waste a miracle.

Part One

ONE
Beginnings

The village of Minden in Haliburton County is nestled in one of the many tourist areas of central Ontario. It was home to a few thousand residents and thousands more seasonal cottagers. The population swelled enormously in the summer. During the wintry months, robust cold weather enthusiasts dotted the frozen lakes, winterized cottages, and snow-covered hills as they skated, skied, sledded, and played hockey. Winter carnivals and dogsled races were also favourite events.

My dad was a small motors mechanic as well as an entrepreneur. I had two older brothers, Morley and Keith, and a younger sister, Joy. She indeed added much joy to our family. I can still see her sitting on Dad's knee on the rocking chair by the wood-burning stove in the kitchen. She was just a toddler, listening intently as Dad sang "You Are My Sunshine."

For a season of time, we had a good number of chickens, a few pigs, and at least two cows. I have many great memories from growing up on our little farm, but my favourite is of a well-mannered but busy pig. Dad couldn't maintain a fence sufficiently to keep him inside an enclosed space, since the pig escaped regularly. He wandered around our property at will, often taking a hike up our country road for a change of scenery. We could always count on him returning to his pen by suppertime, though. He also allowed us to ride him like a horse. What fun we had!

Dad started a business selling and servicing chainsaws, which provided him with lots of work. It was in an era when chainsaws were in high demand. Many men made their living with these devices. Dad could repair anything with a motor, though, so there were always customers coming and going from his shop, locals as well as cottage owners from hither and yon. He often worked late into the evening. We frequently went to sleep to the sound of revving motors.

He was a hard-working man, and my brothers learned the business of repairing motors and maintaining the shop. This stood them in good stead.

Morley spent his adult life in Ecuador and often needed to repair motors of various kinds. He often couldn't find the required parts and had to build them from whatever was available.

Keith eventually took over our dad's business and developed it further. Later in life, he had his own hair salon business. He said it was three months before he got all the grease out of his fingernails.

As Dad's business grew, he also sold and serviced lawn and garden equipment. Next, he added the sale of snow machines. He eventually made a go-kart track on our property, adding another successful summer business. Local enthusiasts and tourist enjoyed our track, as well as nearly county resorts who organized weekly tournaments for their guests.

My brothers weren't pleased that I held the speed record on the track for a few years. They couldn't be convinced it was skill.

"You don't weigh as much as we do," they would say.

One day a small but wiry elderly lady came to our track. At the time she was known as the Racing Grandmother. What a delight it was to meet this lady at the age of ninety-four! She had heard of Dad's business and wanted to check it out. She took a few laps around the track and then gave our dad a nod of approval. We were all impressed.

My mom kept our household humming and taught Joy and I the art of doing so as well.

One chore I could never master was cleaning a chicken. It was not for the lack of her teaching, nor me trying. It just wasn't meant to be.

As a married Bible college student in Alberta many years later, our landlord was given several chickens for his family and his three tenant families. The only cost to us was cleaning these feathery birds. How I wished my mother was there that day!

Mom always worked wonders with freshly picked strawberries, wild blackberries, blueberries, apples, and our garden produce. My dad was a hunter, providing venison meat in our freezer, and often moose meat as well. Mom excelled in the preparation of wild meat to make it so very tasty.

Dad built a smokehouse for pork. We probably ate that well-mannered pig for a whole year. He rented out the smokehouse for neighbours for their pork as well. The smell of smoked bacon often flooded our little valley.

There was a maple bush on our property. Our family all had a part to play when the sap was running in late winter and early spring. Dad and the boys tapped the trees and then everyone helped gather sap. It was a big endeavour, moving from one tree to another the old-fashioned way, emptying each bucket into a large barrel drawn by hand on a sleigh.

Dad, the boys, and I took turns boiling down the sap and taking off the syrup at the right time. My mother finished the process of bottling the maple syrup in our kitchen. We usually still had enough well into the following winter. Every year, we could sell a few gallons for our efforts.

One evening brought an unpleasant turn of events, halting our syrup-making for the year. My girlfriend Shirley and I were on deck to boil down the sap that evening. We built a good fire under the pan of sap that was already boiling and returned to the house to gather some snacks for our shift. Red flag!

While we left the house with our arms full of munchies, giggling as usual, we saw fire on the hill. I raced up the hill as quickly as my legs would take me, screaming for Shirley to alert Dad and the boys. I breathed a hurried prayer.

I remember wondering what I would do when I got there, but I knew I had to try. Fortunately, the boys were right behind and passed me before I reached the fiery pan. They flew into action, quenching the fire. But the pan could not be saved.

That incident is one of those events I wish I could erase from my memory. But lessons were learned!

Dad advertised his business in various ways, at local seasonal fairs and carnivals as well as the Toronto Sportsman Show. We frequently attended these events as a family, but some years we would take turns going with Dad. I loved attending with Dad. It was always a special treat for me when I didn't have to share him.

When Morley, Keith, and I were still young, Dad started his summer work at the nearby Kilcoo Camp. The privileged boys who attended this camp were from the homes of professionals around the Toronto area. A few often came from various places around the United States as well as overseas. It was a well-known facility where campers sharpened their water skills, archery, and other crafts. They also took canoe trips throughout our county, which had hundreds of lakes. The challenging rocks and hills provided opportunities to practice portaging. The wilds of central Ontario had much to offer these campers.

Over several years, Morley and Keith both got involved as campers and counsellors. Morley and another fellow carved a pair of strikingly beautiful totem poles which marked the entrance to Kilcoo for decades.

This was a camp for boys, though. Girls weren't allowed, not even as staff.

In August 1949, some of these boys arrived not feeling well. The parents, assuming their sons were just excited about the upcoming trip, had brought them anyway.

However, they were quickly sent home for treatment. My parents heard later that a few of these boys hadn't survived. Eventually it was revealed that they had contracted polio.

TWO
Polio Strikes Home

The epidemic of '49 was underway. The polio serum was soon to be available... but not yet. In Canada, the serum become available in 1952. Scientists and researchers had been developing this serum for more than a decade before inoculating children. It effectively stopped polio in its tracks.

The polio virus took the lives of thousands of young boys and girls as it raced across Canada over a period of several months. Some survivors were left to spend the rest of their lives in iron lungs while others wore heavy braces or using crutches or other assistive devices. Some survivors dealt with limb deformities, undeveloped muscles, the fear of choking, or respiratory issues. All survivors had to learn how to face the rest of their lives with the various degrees of discomfort, pain, and weakness that accompanied their disabilities.

I was one of those little people in early September of 1949.

My two brothers and I fell ill with what my mother called the worst case of flu-like symptoms she had ever witnessed. My oldest brother Morley, who was eight, remembered this time. We could only get out of our beds to use the washroom, otherwise we basically slept all day and night. He remembered that his legs felt full of water. When he slowly pushed his weakened body to the washroom, he sensed the water sloshing in his legs. As the years went by, he often remarked on this weird, sickening, and horrible experience. He carried the vivid memory for the rest of his life.

At the end of that challenging week, both of my brothers recovered. I did not.

Years later, as a young adult, a chiropractor treated my back. Hearing my history convinced him that I had been more susceptible to the virus due to a back injury I'd sustained from taking a tumble a couple of months prior.

When I still wasn't getting better, my grandmother offered to take me along with her to see her family doctor, since she already had an appointment. This was an era when a person visited the doctor's office only when they were very, very ill or if they required regular follow-up, as was the case for my Grama Miller. We had one doctor for our county at the time, Dr. Agnes Jamieson, and she was well respected. She was an artist as well as a wonderful, no-nonsense family doctor. After Dr. Jamieson retired, her many art pieces were put on display at the local art gallery in Minden. The gallery still carries her name.

On the day of my visit to her office in early September 1949, she diagnosed polio. Arrangements were immediately made to transport me to Toronto Sick Kids Hospital, where it was hoped I would survive, receive treatment, and tolerate rehab.

The memory of the three-hour trip to Toronto escapes me, but I can remember several dramatic events from my ensuing three-and-a-half-month hospitalization. One of those events was a particular test on my back, which I endured while lying on my stomach. This was a spinal tap, a lumbar puncture which, to verify that my illness was indeed polio.

A member of the Toronto Shriners Club came into the room the day of the spinal tap. This grown man lay on the floor, looking up so I could see his pleasant face. It was a welcoming sight, helping me not to feel so afraid in this frightening room where I was otherwise alone with a bunch of doctors and strangers. I was physically uncomfortable and in pain, weak, and unable to walk, run, and play, and I missed my family, but this smiling man introduced himself and called me by my name. That was special.

He had come to tell me a story about a yellow kitten. If the purpose of his visit was to take my mind off the doctor's work, it really worked. I remember the whole story to this day. I don't remember the pain of the lumbar puncture.

The yellow kitten had climbed high into a tree, but he was too afraid to come back down. The kitten's family tried different ways to get him to climb down the same way he had climbed up, but nothing worked. The kitten just sat there, perched firmly on the limb of the tree, and cried with a sad voice.

Finally, the dad called the fire department. I remember wondering why this smiling man told me about the firefighters being on the way. How could they help? There was no fire.

The firefighters arrived with their big red fire truck and set up their long ladder against the high tree. I wondered if the kitten would be afraid of that ladder and try to scamper up even higher.

One of the firefighters climbed up the ladder as the others watched from the ground, assuring the family that everything was going to be okay.

When the brave fireman was close enough, he quietly spoke to the kitten. He carefully reached out his big, friendly hand so the kitten wouldn't be afraid. He then let the fireman pick him up and hold him tight to his chest.

Once the firefighter came back down the long ladder, he gave the kitten to the family. Everyone was so happy that they screamed with delight.

The firefighters went back to their fire station to wait for another call to help someone in need.

My son-in-law Andrew has had a career as a firefighter for more than a quarter of a century. He says that fire departments still receive calls periodically to rescue dogs and kittens from trees—and they still go. Good to know!

As an adult, I took the opportunity to speak with a member of a Shriners Club while they entertained the crowd at a summer fair. He appreciated hearing my story as I thanked him on behalf of girls and boys who had enjoyed their stories over the years in hospitals. He told me that they still go to hospitals when called to help children through tough times. To this day, I have a special place in my heart for firefighters and anyone else who will stoop so low as to help a child.

After three weeks of recovery from the first stage of polio, I was transferred to Thistletown Rehabilitation Hospital in the northern part of Toronto. This was a very different setting for me. My parents were able to visit for two hours on Sunday afternoons, but only every second week. How lonely and sad I often felt, crying myself to sleep at nights.

One Sunday afternoon, my parents visited but weren't allowed to come inside. As young patients, we didn't know why and couldn't understand this. The large hospital cribs in our huge room were pushed closer to the big wall of bright windows, though, and I remember struggling to sit up in bed, searching to find my mom and dad in the sea of faces on the other side.

Finally, I saw them and waved. That's all we could do that Sunday. Just wave. They couldn't hold us in their arms. They couldn't tell us how much they loved us and missed us. They couldn't tell us what was going on at home with our siblings and pets. They couldn't bring any treats. And we couldn't show them what we were able to do since their last visit.

Tears stung my cheeks that night as I finally went off to sleep. The memory of this remains fresh in my mind. I really missed my mom. I wanted her often, but I needed her especially that night.

Later in life, as each of my four children reached that same age when I remember needing my mom so desperately, memories flooded my mind. I would cling to my child at bedtime. They seemed so small and it was difficult to imagine them being taken away from me, like I had been taken away from my mom at that age for so many months.

Tears sometimes flow freely. Even as I write this many years later, a sensation swells up in my chest and moves into my throat. And yes, here is a tear.

Two important factors from this time affected my life forever.

First, I had a praying grandmother. She immediately prayed that I would survive. She prayed for the hospital staff who cared for my needs. She prayed for God's loving comfort regarding the lonely hours I experienced. She prayed for my parents in my absence from their home. She prayed for my brothers, who of course wouldn't admit that they missed me, but Grama knew better. She prayed that I would grow into a young lady who recognized God's presence in my life and accepted His miracle of salvation. She prayed that I would have a productive, happy, and meaningful adult life, making a difference and impacting lives for Christ.

She covered so many bases. I wouldn't be writing these words today were it not for God's work through my praying grandmother.

I have taken a page from my grandmother's book with regards to praying for my grandchildren. At the time of this writing, four are in their twenties and three are in their young teenage years. I am privileged to pray for each one.

Secondly, I learned that children die. In the large rehab ward, we would sometimes wake up to an empty bed in the morning. The very large room was filled with children recovering from polio in various stages.

The nurses no doubt performed their duties in a discreet manner, but when we saw an empty bed we knew that another new friend had died in the night. That friend hadn't gone home like we all wanted.

When kids went home, they left in the daytime with at least one parent. We could all say goodbye to them and be reminded that our day would soon come.

But when we saw those empty beds, we knew they were gone forever…. passed away, dead, no more to be seen.

That's how I remember describing death when I found a lifeless baby chick or bird or squirrel on our family farm.

Yes, my hospital experience moulded me into the adult I eventually became. I learned to acknowledge and accept the loss of loved ones, recognizing the cycle of friendship, whether it lasts for a few weeks or a lifetime. I came to appreciate life and the people in our lives, choosing to live every day as if it could be my last, knowing that sometimes not even doctors, nurses, and therapists can help.

There are three types of polio. I had bulbar poliomyelitis and had experienced some paralysis. Relearning motor skills and learning to walk again was first and foremost in my recovery plan. The physiotherapists drilled the message to us loud and clear: "Use it or you will lose it."

Even as a young child, I gradually came to understand what these words meant.

The sight of one physical therapist remains etched in my mind. He stood tall in his white pants and white shirt, often with his large hands on his hips. I remember that he didn't seem as gentle and kind as some of the other physical therapists, who were careful and motherly in the way they talked to us. He stood close and looked straight down at me as I tried to stay on my unsteady feet while clinging to the bars.

"It doesn't matter that it hurts," he said. "Ignore the pain. It doesn't matter that it hurts."

I didn't even know what the word *ignore* meant at the time, but he was right: it did hurt. These experiences made me even more determined to complete his hurtful exercises... if it meant I could go home one day with Mom and Dad and not die.

After a few months, I was strong enough to shed the heavy, ugly brace on my right leg and was able to carefully walk on my own. It still hurt, but I did it.

Eventually I stopped falling. I could move myself around that big exercise room... well, almost. There were always lots of adults clad in their white uniforms if anyone got in trouble and needed help. I no longer had to be pushed in a cute little wheelchair, though. I could walk.

I still wasn't allowed to get out of my crib by myself and take a walk around our large room. A kind nurse explained that I still needed someone with me in case something happened. Also, she said I needed to get much stronger. I thought I was already strong.

I remember the day when I walked out of that rehab hospital with Mom and Dad on either side of me, saying goodbye to my new friends while tightly clasping my little hands in theirs. I was going home just in time for Christmas!

It turned out that Dad's business had suffered somewhat during my time in the hospital. Many of his customers had been too afraid of polio to bring their chainsaws or motors to his shop for repair. Some braver souls left their motors at the end of the driveway and picked them up there afterward.

People also stopped buying eggs from Mom and it took many months to build up her sales again. Neither of my parents had been able to shop in town for food and do their regular errands. Their groceries got delivered to the end of our driveway. The boys hadn't been able to start school after my hospitalization, either. My family was in seclusion.

THREE
Moving Along with Life at Home

Our family life gradually returned to normal again.

Following my hospital stay, there was a six-month recovery. My mom religiously made me do the exercises that had been sent home from Dr. Mustard, Toronto's main polio doctor. I thought they were a waste of time, robbing me of the opportunity to play. In hindsight, though, I'm thankful that Mom insisted I follow them to a T.

One ridiculous exercise involved a pail of sand. Mom would hide a dozen marbles throughout the sand and my goal was to use the toes of my right foot to find and retrieve them.

At the beginning, this took a lot of time. The exercise hurt. The frail and scrawny muscle in my leg was very weak. My ankle and foot were stiff, weak, and wobbly.

Within a few months, though, my leg and little toes did regain some strength and the exercise took less and less time. It eventually even became fun. I did that exercise twice every day for six months.

Dr. Mustard also prescribed several hours of rest every day. That pill was much harder to swallow than the pill of exercise. With exercise I was at least active and not confined to my bed. The challenge of resting so much made me get creative with books, dolls, small toys, games, music, paper and pencil, colouring, and anything else that could occupy my mind and allow me to remain horizontal. Apparently, lying flat in bed allowed my muscles to innervate.

My mom understood what Dr. Mustard wanted, and my work was to do what they both agreed on. I remember not ever wanting to sleep in the daytime, and that hasn't changed. To this day, if I sleep in the daytime, I'm not well.

We celebrated my fifth birthday in January. My mom wasn't into having big birthday parties, but rather the birthday child could have one friend over for the afternoon and later our family dinner. Mom made our favourite meal, which was always followed by chocolate birthday cake. She often made chocolate cakes, but the chocolate birthday cakes had more icing and were beautifully decorated. The icing was lavished on the top, over the sides, and between the layers. There were candles on top, of course, and sometimes we found pennies inside, wrapped in foil.

We never felt we were missing anything in our home with such celebrations. Mom made our birthdays feel special.

As a side note, the Canadian penny in the mid-1900s was a gift worth receiving. If a child wanted to buy "penny candy," it didn't take many to have a whole handful of sweet treats that would last for days, maybe even weeks.

School finally started for me in September 1950. I was thrilled. I loved to learn new things, read, take a packed lunch, and play with friends. Throughout my school career, spelling was my best subject. I detested science. History wasn't a favourite, either. Math was okay. I really enjoyed music, though, and I especially enjoyed Geography. I loved studying the huge map of the world that hung on the wall beside the beautiful picture of Queen Elizabeth at the front of our little red schoolhouse.

I became fascinated with the country of Australia on the bottom right-hand side of that map. I was also intrigued at the vastness of Russia. I often wondered what it would be like to visit those two countries… well, to visit anywhere outside the little dot where we lived in Ontario. I was curious about what mountains looked like, how tall they were, what could grow on them, what the prairies were like, and what kind of vehicles raced along the roads. Did the children have bikes in other places? Were their homes like ours? I had so many questions.

I had such a strong desire to visit other places, but how could it ever be possible? How could I travel with this gimpy leg attached to my weakened body? I often needed extra rest.

I was a daydreamer, however, and found myself learning about these other countries. By reading about them for myself, I was able to "travel" everywhere, meeting people from a variety of cultures, tasting their food, flying in airplanes, and riding foreign cars, trains, and even elephants! I walked amidst mountains and checked out jungles.

By staring at maps, I would choose a pretend flight, then imagine the roads I would take to visit these countries and their people. My favourite book was my world atlas, which I received more than seventy years ago now. It still occupies a space on my bookshelf. Tattered, torn, and full of scribbles, it remains a special book to me. Over the years, I've bought two newer atlases, but my old atlas still comes out when I really want to visit the pages of a country.

Back to reality, though.

I was able to be a flower girl at my Uncle Floyd's wedding in the fall of 1950. His bride had gotten a yellow satin dress made for me to wear that day. How special that long, beautiful dress was! I wore it with pride, feeling like a princess. It was good for my young heart.

The challenge, as always, was to find a pair of shoes that looked appropriate for such an occasion. Something that wouldn't make me look so much like an oddball as my sturdy, supportive, often ugly black oxfords did. At least, that's how I felt about my shoes in those years.

During my first year in school, my Uncle Ray was in eighth grade. All the grades occupied the same room. It wasn't a big school, but that was normal for the era. I was so proud to have my Uncle Ray in school with me. He was a fun uncle, and it seemed like he always kept an eye open for me. I suspect his mother, my Grama Miller, had told him to.

One day I jumped off a big rock while playing with a couple Grade One kids during the lunch hour. I either misjudged where I would land or didn't have enough oomph to propel myself as far as I planned. Whatever the reason, I landed on a spiky twig of some sort of bush. A sliver of wood rammed into the scrawny muscle of my right leg. It hurt like the dickens!

The other kids didn't know what to do with me. Seeing the blood spurt out, I thought I should holler for help, but before I could actually do it my Uncle Ray was right there. He scooped me up and placed me on the big rock like I was a sack of sugar. He gently pulled that sliver straight out. More blood gushed and assured me I would be fine as he carried me into the schoolhouse.

I remember our teacher being very grandmotherly. She cleaned the wounded area and covered it with a cool, soothing ointment. She then wrapped some gauze and bandage around my leg to stop the blood from running out. How I loved that teacher.

At our little red schoolhouse, the total count of students maxed out at thirty-two in grades One through Eight, although some years had fewer. We all played baseball in late spring and early fall. This sport was instrumental in teaching skill, patience, and cooperation, according to our teacher.

I grew accustomed to being the last kid chosen for a team. Running certainly wasn't my strength, and my lack of coordination hampered any skill I might have had to hit the ball where it should go. But every student had to have a turn on a team throughout the day, and most students cooperated. Some thought I was a nuisance.

Baseball was never the highlight of my day, although it served as another character-building exercise.

As I got older, my right leg didn't grow as fast as the rest of me. My right foot was deformed and the calf didn't develop properly. The right leg got even more gimpy and tardy when my body grew tired. My back knew pain far too often. My breathing was shallow and my left arm weak. I was a hurting unit.

It became difficult to keep my feet warm and comfortable, and we spent more money on my shoes and winter boots than for both of my brothers together. My parents grew accustomed to my foot bill through the years while I was under their roof. Of course, they were happy that I had recovered sufficiently to even face this challenge.

I always wore sturdy, supportive oxfords, even in hot weather when my friends skipped about in their bare feet.

During the cold winter months, I required boots with room for more than one pair of warm socks, yet they had to be supportive and comfortable enough to keep me moving and as active as possible.

The only shoe store owner in town became my friend. His name was Mr. Welsh. He was kind to me and would take the time to search around his store to find just what my parents thought would best suit my needs for each season.

In my second year of high school, I was referred to a podiatrist in Peterborough. His name was Dr. Foote. Yes, my foot specialist was Dr. Foote! His father had also been a podiatrist in Toronto, and his brother was the editor of our local newspaper in Minden. Dr. Foote became my friend and I saw him regularly for several decades.

He recommended specially made "space shoes." These shoes were well named; they were indeed out of this world. The right shoe was made to accommodate my unique foot. It was built up higher to accommodate my shorter right leg.

I have to admit that these space shoes provided comfort for my hurting foot, aching leg, and painful back. My habit was not to complain, but deep inside I wished for the day when I wouldn't have to wear those ugly space shoes. The only consolation was that they weren't black. Since they were custom-made, they could be ordered in different colours. I insisted on beige and my parents went along with my desire.

By the time I turned thirteen, I was asked to sing at my Uncle Ray's wedding, along with my brother Morley and a niece of the bride. We sang our hearts out, presenting two hymns at their lovely wedding. I was thrilled to later have a part in a second wedding.

FOUR
1957–1958

I bought my first bicycle in the spring of 1957 when I was in Grade Seven. I had just turned twelve in January and the price of the bike was twelve dollars. I remember saving my birthday money, as well as money I earned doing extra chores at home and for my grandmother.

Our parents were of the opinion that their children should earn money to buy special items like a bicycle. They had both lived through the Depression and worked hard during the post-war years to make a life for their family. They'd learned how to live without unnecessary items, as well as appreciate the value of hard work. They taught each of their children those same values. As a result, I appreciated my bike!

My grandparents lived three miles from our home, and in good summer weather I biked there as often as I could, stopping halfway to visit my best friend, Shirley. Sometimes she was allowed to ride alongside me on her own bike. What simple fun we had spending time together on our bikes, laughing, and enjoying warm homemade cookies in Grama's big happy farm kitchen. She always gave us cookies for the ride home, too.

Shirley and I sometimes helped Grampa in the hayfield. Of course, we each had chores to do at home as well.

The summer of 1957 was my last so-called carefree summer, and it became a favourite of mine. Starting the next summer, I began working.

For the next three summers, I was a helper for two young children from Monday through Friday in July and August. I boarded with that family and returned home for weekends.

For the following three summers, I ventured off to a Christian conference camp where I lived and worked.

After that, I worked for my parents' business.

Working in the summers added to my many character-building experiences.

I began high school in September 1958. At the time, we lived about nineteen miles from the school in nearby Haliburton. It was a one-hour bus ride. Those were the days when girls still wore skirts or dresses to school, often with white and navy lace-up saddle shoes with white bobby socks. In my parent's eyes, they qualified as sturdy oxfords, so I started high school in style!

The other popular style of girls shoes was brown penny loafers. I surely would have liked to wear a pair of those, but they didn't work for me.

One day following a regular gym class, I asked the girl in the next shower if playing volleyball hurt her body, too. She was surprised that I would ask such a question. As we talked, I realized that I was indeed a hurting unit, unlike the other students.

Eventually my doctor provided a note excusing me from actual participation in high school sports. By then I required pain medication periodically and those ugly space shoes became a regular part of my wardrobe. I had enjoyed dressing in style for only a short time with those white and blue saddle shoes.

Had my determination to get on with life not been made so strong by my early hospital stay and recovery, those ugly space shoes would have been a total embarrassment to me. But I accepted them since they would help me move on in life and reduce my pain and discomfort. Some students made fun of them. Others were curious as to how I could even wear them. Still others accepted them as I did, knowing that they made my life a bit more comfortable.

FIVE
Issues of the Heart and Soul

Bitterness crept into my heart as I watched my friends get involved in skating, skiing, dancing, running, sports, and hiking. None of them required extra rest, which made me feel different.

My grandmother knew how to talk with me about anything, though. We often baked together in her farm kitchen while talking about all manner of things. She shared her faith in God. We also talked about my growing bitterness.

She was also very perceptive and always knew when something was bothering me. One evening while at her home, a raging thunderstorm frightened me terribly. She calmed my spirit, always knowing what to say.

The bottom line is that my grandmother told me it wasn't necessary to be angry with God because my circumstances made me feel different than everyone else. She reminded me how fortunate I was to be alive and looking forward to new opportunities in my teenage years.

On the day we addressed my bitterness issue, I came to understand that God was real and anxious for me to get to know Him. I believe it was God who removed my bitterness. I learned that when He does something in our lives, the work is done.

That bitterness has never resurfaced. For that, I'm thankful. What a great way to begin my teens!

In April 1958, our church brought in some special speakers in Rev. and Mrs. J. Allan Wallace. They served with Faith Mission of Canada and had come from Great Britain some three decades previously. Their mission was to share the love of God, and they certainly did that!

Their evangelistic services were held in many areas of the province. They worked with children, camps, and ministries for both women and men. They held Sunday services and assisted with midweek programs. The mission also held dinners and served people in many practical ways. Our church in Minden was privileged and blessed to host them for several days.

During one service, I felt God tug at my heart and inner spirit. They were discussing John 3:16, which convicted my young heart. The truth of this one verse was made so clear by Rev. Wallace. I have since heard this verse referred to as the Gospel in a nutshell, and indeed that was true for me that April evening.

Allow me to paraphrase John 3:16 from my understanding. The verse says that God loves everyone in the world so very much that He sent His only Son, Jesus Christ, to this earth. Jesus not only taught how to live, but how to love. He then gave His life for us all. This was indeed good news!

I drank in the truth. Jesus had given up His life for me, you, and everyone. The Bible describes how He allowed men to nail Him to a cross, where He shed His blood, dying for our sin. We have all sinned. Not even one of us on this earth is perfect.

There is a condition, though, which is our responsibility, because God never forces Himself on anyone.

Here I am! I stand at the door and knock. If anyone hears my voice and opens the door, I will come in and eat with that person, and they with me. (Revelation 3:20)

I once found a painting which depicts the image shared in this verse. In it, Jesus stands at a beautiful garden door, knocking. The door represents the door of our hearts, of our lives. There is no handle or doorknob. In other words, it is our choice to open the door to Jesus. We must open it from the inside and ask Him to come in. He doesn't barge in. He is a gentleman.

Whoever believes this is eternally saved. Believers will indeed have eternal life with God forever. When we believe what God provided us through His only Son Jesus, and when we are done on this earth—as in, when we die—we will go to be with God.

Many verses in the Bible say that we will go to the place He has prepared for us: heaven. For how long? John 3:16 says that it will be forever.

At the church that day in April 1958, my heart raced. I believed.

Not quite understanding this newfound release, I sought out Rev. Wallace after the service. We talked. He prayed. I prayed. I then thanked God, asking His forgiveness for anything I had done or thought that was against Him and His teaching in the Bible. Remorse filled my soul in the light of His awesome love and holiness.

I accepted His forgiveness. I gave God my life! A wonderful cleansing and wholeness came over me. They could only have come from God, for no one could conjure up those feelings.

I thanked God and praised Him for who He is and what He had provided through His Son. The Holy Spirit had done His job at drawing me to God the Father.

This was all so clear, yet also overwhelming. I revelled in what had just happened.

Salvation gave my life purpose. My decision didn't alter the physical pain and weakness in my body, but it did give me direction to live for and serve our wonderful God, our heavenly Father. It was like I made an about-face. I had been going in a direction away from God, and then I turned and moved toward Him.

It was an eye-opener for me. He knew my physical challenges. He knew my desires.

The experience brought clarity and understanding to what my grandmother had often shared. I now understood where she had been coming from. Wow! Jesus really was the reason for the season when we celebrated Christmas. He really was the gift! And as with any gift, it was up to us to accept it. We only needed to believe, confess, and accept.

My life changed. My participation in Sunday services became more meaningful. The activity in our church youth group took on a new dimension.

I was soon given the opportunity to assist in a children's Sunday school class. The midweek Bible study and prayer meeting also became the focal point of my week. I was introduced to the wonderful world of prayer, a whole new dimension which has become an important part of my life to this day.

I visited Rev. Wallace again later in life, in 1996. He was quite elderly and his wife had recently passed. I found him sitting in a comfortable chair in a senior's residence, a warm cover over his thin legs and an open Bible on his lap.

His mind was as sharp as a tack. He remembered being in Minden in the spring of 1958 and the good number of teens who had either renewed their commitment to God or become believers that week. He asked whether I knew what they were doing now, mentioning that they must all be in their fifties by that time. I shared as much as I knew of each of these young people.

He was delighted to hear the report, although he was also saddened to hear that two of the young men had recently died at fifty-one and fifty-three years of age. He rejoiced, though, to hear of how they had served God.

What a privilege it was to be able to spend that hour with Rev. Wallace thirty years after I first met him. The time flew and we finished in prayer. It was an honour to hear this man pray after having served God in such a powerful way for more than seventy of his ninety-some years.

SIX
Murray Wesley Sisson

Murray was always known as a shy, gentle-spoken man. Don't get me wrong; he could get upset. If you were in earshot and heard him say "Boys oh boys oh boys," you'd know something had upset him, and it wasn't necessarily his boys. I never heard him utter a traditional swear word in the thirty-nine years I knew him. He lived wholesomely and I fell desperately and deeply in love with him at the age of thirteen.

Did I mention he was handsome?

In his late thirties, he grew a full beard. The colour eventually turned silver and he looked like a million dollars, especially in his steel grey suit.

When he decided to grow that beard, it mostly because he was tired of his daily shaving routine. So he declared that he'd wear the beard until he shot his first buck in the annual November deer hunt. That beard looked good on that face of his right from the start. He kept it well trimmed and we all grew accustomed to the look. Most thought he was even more handsome!

Debra-Kaye had a difficult time adjusting to the beard on her dad's face, though.

As the years went by, he would shoot a couple of does in November. However, the buck kept evading him. Ten years passed. The beard thrived.

Then, one crisp November morning, a magnificent buck came out to his watch. Murray was sure he could take him down, but he hesitated for just a moment as he took aim. The deer stood tall on a slight knoll and then looked directly at this hunter with a gun to his shoulder.

In that moment, Murray realized that taking the life of this buck would mean shaving off his ten-year-old beard.

He shot. He shaved. It was the one and only beard he ever grew.

Murray's family regularly attended church. Their lifestyle, attitudes, and behaviours were indeed wholesome. He accepted Jesus and gave his life to God at the tender age of five.

He and his four younger siblings were raised on a farm a few miles outside Minden. Their lives were busy with planting and harvesting, caring for horses and a herd of beef cattle, cutting wood for heat, and making hundreds of gallons of maple syrup. His dad worked full-time for Ontario Hydro to keep the farm running.

They were a typical farm family. The four boys helped outside, and their sister Ruth helped their mom inside. An uncle to Murray's dad also lived with the family and worked around the farm.

Murray and I first met when he was fourteen and I was twelve. I had known of his family for several years, however. His maternal grandfather had married one of my maternal grandfather's sisters. Both were in their late twenties at the time and six children were born to them, five boys and one girl. Murray's half-uncles and half-aunt were my third cousins.

One can imagine the challenge, years down the road, of explaining to our four children how they were twice related to those relatives. I always rested in the fact that Murray and I weren't blood-related.

Many years later, after Murray's mom and my dad had passed, his dad and my mom dated for seven years. They often attended the same senior's dinners, church, and community events, so they decided that they may as well travel together. When they discovered that they enjoyed each other's company, the courtship began.

They soon looked, and acted, ten years younger. They were even engaged to be married at some point, though they changed their minds and just remained friends, he on his farm three miles north of Minden and Mom in her little bungalow on the flat three miles south of

Minden. Had they married, Murray and I would have become brother and sister… and our children? Well, they would have been cousins to each other. We would have been uncle and aunt to our own children!

Murray and I started our sporadic period of dating when I was eighteen. We married when I was six months past twenty-one and Murray had recently celebrated his twenty-fourth birthday. Those three years were filled with travelling for summer jobs, me working a year in Toronto, Murray's employment with Ontario Hydro in Minden, not to mention his study at Prairie Bible College in Alberta. This didn't leave much time for serious dating, since we were rarely in the same place, but it was another good character-building exercise.

One of those years, however, we were both students at Prairie. The school had an extremely strict social regulation in the 1960s, though. Students couldn't date. The founder of the school, Mr. Maxwell, believed that students needed to commit to study for an eight-month period; there would be time for dating later.

Since then, the school's social regulations have relaxed, as well as other areas of disciplines.

I remember sneaking off campus on a pleasant spring-like evening in late March just as the sun was setting on the vast prairie horizon. Murray and I met in the town's graveyard. Two other couples were involved that evening. The three boys had devised the plan, and of course we girls went along with it. Who would ever think to look in a graveyard for students, should we be missed from campus for an hour? I will only confess to the fact that we were pleased with ourselves, though we had broken regulations.

Even in the sixties, the church youth group in Minden was a hopping place. Murray was there on Friday evenings, as was I when at home. Activities included games of various sorts, competitions, outings, and meaningful Bible studies. Our teen church lives also involved sports, concerts, and youth conferences. There were also hayrides in the summer and sleighrides in the winter and fundraisers for worthy projects. We often assisted seniors with spring or fall cleaning. We also organized banquets, picnics, and meals together. Our lives were very busy.

One of my good friends was Esther, one of our pastor's six children.

Pastor Schmitt had a great rapport with children and teens. My first memory of him was coming to our little red schoolhouse for a class on religious instruction, which was permissible back in the day.

He and his family held services in different homes in the county, as well as at our school on Sunday evenings. Eventually there were enough families to support a building and ministry in Minden.

Murray's family was one of them. When the church opened in Minden, my brothers and I began attending Sunday mornings as well as the youth program... and there was Murray.

Pastor Schmitt was instrumental in encouraging people to personally read and study the Bible. His wife Ruth became a spiritual mentor, encouraging me particularly in the ministry of music and prayer. I remember her favourite saying: "Keep your nose in the Book." She was a beautiful singer and musician, too, giving me pointers as an organist. She also made sweet music on her accordion. She tried to give me lessons on the accordion, but alas, it was very heavy; my upper torso didn't have the strength to hold it, nor the coordination to make music on that instrument.

Esther and I both worked at a Christian conference camp for two summers. After high school, we roomed together for a year in Toronto, and she was my maid of honour when Murray and I married. She eventually married Larry and they lived in Toronto. We supported one another as often as we could when our six children were babies and preschoolers. After their move to western Canada, however, our visits have waned.

The Minden church was considered a small-town church, with a membership averaging in the thirties for many years. Attendance swelled in the summer months as tourists came to the various cottages, campgrounds, and resorts. There was standing room only sometimes during the summer, yet people kept coming.

Most church-going people attended and supported a local church during their vacations in that era. Families with children were anxious to have their Sunday school attendance cards stamped for their home Sunday school attendance contests.

Our youth program averaged sixty teens every Friday evening, fifty weeks of the year. We had dedicated youth leaders who loved us and gave of their time and talents, and often from their own wallets, to provide the program. They truly cared for our spiritual needs as well as our overall development into wholesome young men and women. Participation in our youth group complemented our home and school training in preparation for entering secular and Christian fields of work.

Murray was one of the finest employees of Ontario Hydro during his career. For fourteen years, he also served on a committee for Men for Missions,[2] visiting and supporting Christian mission activity in Ecuador. He was able to make five trips to that part of South America.

Here are a few other facts about Murray. He was often called on to preach in church services in different seasons of his life. He also cheered endlessly and faithfully for the Toronto Maple Leafs! He eventually upgraded his four-year diploma from Prairie to an accredited degree. Later in life he played community baseball and hockey, taught a variety of Bible studies, and served on community ministerial committees. He was a care provider for me, too, whenever possible, during my seven years as a full-time power wheelchair driver. He was my constant.

Murray was diagnosed with ulcerative colitis at the age of nineteen, having one major surgery twenty-nine years later.

Within a few years of that surgery, cancer spread through his body. He was gone at the age of fifty-three. Seven hundred people paid their respects during his visitation and funeral. Five of his clergy friends from hither and yon took part in the funeral service.

Family and friends emotionally supported me and the children during those days. Murray's life had attracted laypeople and professionals from both secular and Christian communities. I still miss him!

---

[2] Men for Missions (MFM) is the laymen's arm of OMS International, a mission which we supported for many years.

SEVEN
Mister and Missus

A fine day it was in early September 1966. Our little country church was decorated with seasonal flowers as Murray and I exchanged vows, committing our lives to each other and promising to serve the Lord together. Ours was the traditional church wedding, complete with music, decorated vehicles, and everyone dressed in their finery. Family and friends from hither and yon attended our lawn reception with lots of children running about.

As we drove away from our reception that evening, we eventually smelled fried onions. What? Where was this delicious aroma coming from? I wondered about this as we drove further along the country road.

It was a wedding prank, as it turned out. Someone had placed onions on the intake manifold. No doubt the guilty party was a member of the wedding party.

Five months after our wedding, Murray and I travelled with Uncle Elvin, Aunt Ruby. and my sister to Wisconsin for the marriage of our brother Morley to his sweetheart Darlene. Murray and I were expecting our first baby, to be born the end of July. I was doing fine and knew I was up for the trip.

The wedding was lovely, and once the newly married couple had left for their honeymoon we started driving back to Ontario on Sunday morning. The weather had turned frigid over the weekend, however. While driving into the northwest part of Ontario, the early morning temperature hit -52°F. Snappy!

Upon arriving at Uncle Elvin's home, where we had left our car, my cousins informed us that our winterized cottage had burnt to the ground due to an electrical problem. What a shock! Hearing this news, the first words that came out of my mouth were these: "The Lord gave, and the Lord has taken away."

What? The words surprised me, too. They had to have come from God as a reminder that we tried to absorb as the days moved along. Our earthly possessions were of lesser importance to us as we spent the rest of our lives together.

Those words come from Job 1:21. The last part of the verse says, *"May the name of the Lord be praised."*

The Bible relates that Job and his wife had seven sons and three daughters. He was a very wealthy man, a good living man, upright and blameless before God. Job 1:3 says, *"He was the greatest man among all the people of the East."* He had many people in his employ to care for his thousands of sheep, camels, oxen, and donkeys.

Within a few short days, Job lost everything. Everything! Including his children, staff, animals, and wealth.

Job 1 is referred to as Job's first test. Yes, only his first test, for there were more to come. This book presents the awesome story of a man who dedicated himself to living for God, no matter the circumstances.

After many more trials, Job 42 gives him a happy ending, telling of how God blessed the latter end of Job's life even more than its beginning. He was blessed with twice as much as he had before in wealth, workers, and animals. He also had another seven sons and three daughters, living to see grandchildren.

Murray and I had only lost our earthly possessions after the fire. In the days ahead, I thought about the fact that the electrical problem which sparked the blaze could have happened anytime when we were home, including while we were sleeping or while I was home alone during the day. We praised God for His protection and provision in the months that followed, and for the lesson of keeping our priorities straight regarding our earthly possessions.

We praised the name of the Lord.

The Sunday evening we got home from that wedding, I lay in the comfort of my husband's arms. The reality of the fire hit me and tears stung my eyes.

"We will be all right," he gently whispered. "God knows. We'll be all right."

The following morning, my body went into shock. There was concern that I could lose the baby. But after a few rough weeks, the baby and I both stabilized.

The community of Minden came together to support us. Family provided housing and daily necessities. Our bowling team gave us practical household items. A local clothing store provided a substantial gift card, as did the grocery store where we shopped. Our church had a shower for us. We were loved and blessed!

Donna-Lee was born in late July, full-term but very tiny. She weighed in at three pounds, fourteen ounces, a precious little bundle of excitement from the Lord. When she was three weeks old, her weight was up to five pounds—the magic number to be able to bring her home. Thus ended her first extended stay in hospital.

Fifty-four years later, her hospital stay would be much longer.

"Home" was my parents' house south of Minden. Mom and Dad were in Muskoka for the summer where they operated their second go-kart track.

In early September Murray, Donna-Lee, and I drove to Alberta for Murray's third year of study at Prairie Bible College. Donna-Lee was seven weeks old the day she arrived for her first experience on a Bible college campus. She weighed seven pounds that day. She was still a very tiny person.

Following that year of study, we returned to Ontario and lived again in my parents' home while Murray continued his work for Ontario Hydro.

Meanwhile, our second child was well on his way. Dwight was born in late September. A strong little fellow, he had a normal birth weight and soon caught up to his sister, who was growing slowly. They were like a pair of twins for a couple of years.

Murray returned to Prairie that fall, a few weeks late to start his fourth year, while I remained at my parents with our two children. I had a few health complications following Dwight's birth and appreciated the help of my parents and sister. Joy was a fun aunt and a big help for me.

It was a joyous December day when we met Murray at a nearby train station as he returned for Christmas. I have a picture of Dwight lying beside his dad on the bed as a three-month-old, their heads on the same pillow. They each had their opposite hand under their head and wore the same grin on their faces. Murray was getting to know his son. How precious!

The next two weeks were busy with family celebrations as well as packing so the four of us could fly to Alberta for the following four months.

The next joyous occasion came in April with Murray's graduation. My mom and her sister-in-law travelled west for the event. It was a delight to have them with us. The Lubricks, who had been filling in nicely for our parents and a grandma for Donna-Lee, opened their home for Mom and Aunt Marg. They were pampered and fed like queens.

I often revisit memories of the years we spent on the Prairie campus. They bring much joy to my soul, including our first trip to the mountains when we visited Banff. So many good friends came into our lives during this time and stayed for years to come. They were God's special blessings.

Returning to Minden in late April 1969 brought us the opportunity to build our own home on Horseshoe Lake Road, near Murray's parents' farm.

Our third child, Debra-Kaye, was born on an early winter morning the following February. She was a happy little soul and brought more joy to our family.

My labour had started the afternoon before her birth. Fresh snow fell all day and continued into the night.

A young fellow in his twenties was making a food delivery to us in the late afternoon. He knocked on the front door, unhappy about having to stay parked on the road and carry the boxes over the snow-covered driveway. He asked if he could use the toboggan that he saw in the breezeway.

I was somewhat distressed myself, since I was in labour, and in fact I explained that I might need him to drive me to the hospital! He hurried right along, trudging through our snowy driveway with the boxes on our toboggan, making two trips. He then scurried on down the road as quick as his truck would take him.

I think I scared him terribly. He obviously wanted nothing to do with the delivery of a new baby on his watch.

Murray arrived home from work soon. I knew he would sufficiently deal with the driveway to get me to the hospital pronto… which he did. He was a good man!

With Dean's birth in July 1971, our family was complete. He was a sweet little lad and a true last-born, often revealed in his entertaining antics.

The four children were a handful indeed. Busy! Our property became the hub for their cousins and other neighbourhood kids. We had a large backyard with a bit of a hill and many trees. Murray created a picnic area at the top of that hill, a landing spot for snacks, lunches, cool drinks, and homemade cookies.

Our Four D's in 1973.
Front: Donna-Lee and Dean. Back: Dwight and Debra-Kaye.

Two of my sisters-in-law, Sharon and Sylvia, often came for coffee or tea. Their two girls and three boys, respectively, made our home their second home. It was good for the cousins to grow up together in the same neighbourhood.

Donna-Lee wouldn't answer to any name other than Donna-Lee when she was young. As she arrived home on the bus, having had her first day to school, she burst into tears.

"My teacher called me Donna."

I shed a tear too, sensing her sadness, and assured her I would talk with her teacher. The note I sent the next day corrected the misunderstanding. From that day on, she was always addressed as Donna-Lee at school.

My dad had difficulty calling her both names. He said she was just too small to have such a long name.

When she was older, she also answered to DL. And when Dwight was learning to talk, he called her Na. That was an in-house name. I still find myself calling her Na at times.

Debra-Kaye would answer to anything that resembled her given initials—Debbie-Kaye, DK, Debra-Kaye, Deb, and Deborah. A special family friend named her Special K. My dad called her Debbie.

When Dean was learning to talk, he called her Debbie-Pail. One day she had enough of that name, took him by his shirt, and pinned him against the fridge. "Dean, I know you can say 'Debbie-Pail,' and I know you can say 'Okay,' so that means you can say my name right. It's Debbie-Kaye."

"Okay, Debbie-Pail."

That's all it took, though. After that, Debbie-Pail was history.

Our boys were always called Dwight and Dean, and they were happy with them. Their dad had come up with the names given to our children, and I was pleased with each one.

Murray continued working for Ontario Hydro and I was indeed a busy mom. Caring for our home and four little kids was a good exercise for the body. As time went on, though, I often needed a few days of solid rest to keep going. Our children knew how to help with everyday household work and Murray was very supportive. Our parents and friends often lent a helping hand when needed, too, and together we moved through those busy years.

Because of the weakness in my back, hips, and legs from polio, I had trouble bending over. Getting the kids into their snowsuits could be especially challenging. I would have to sit on the floor as they came to me one at a time for help. It was a lengthy process, but we had fun. When everyone was ready, I would scoot or crawl to a chair or cupboard to pull myself up, then grab my own coat, boots, mitts, and hat before heading off. I wouldn't trade those years for anything!

There was a season of time when a few days of rest wasn't enough. My body caved one cold January day in 1974 and I ended up in the local hospital. Arrangements had to be made to transfer me to Toronto General Hospital for a complete assessment.

While waiting in Minden for the ambulance, I began questioning God. Why was this happening to me? I had responsibilities between the young children, my husband, and our home. But it had been getting difficult for me to make a cup of tea for myself, much less hold and drink it. My body was beyond exhausted.

This was the first time I heard God speak directly to me: *"Read Psalm 50."*

I reached for my Bible and turned to the correct chapter.

The Mighty One, God, the Lord, speaks and summons the earth from the rising of the sun to where it sets. From Zion, perfect in beauty, God shines forth. Our God comes and will not be silent... (Psalm 50:1–3)

At this point, I stopped and asked God why He had asked me to read this. I have since asked His forgiveness for being so brash as to question such a specific request. That day, I didn't seem to spot any encouragement or answers from these first few verses.

"Keep reading."

I continued to read, struggling to concentrate. The verses were descriptive, talking about God's greatness and how the heavens declare His righteousness. The passage says that we listen to what God has to say. They speak to His creation of animals and birds. For all this, we are to be thankful.

Nothing new was jumping out at me—that is, until I got to verse fifteen: *"and call on me in the day of trouble; I will deliver you, and you will honor me."*

Well, that got my attention. It surely did! I was in trouble, but God was promising to deliver. My part was to glorify and praise Him. I needed to hear that.

The rest of Psalm 50 goes on to talk about people who ignore God's instruction and lists the awful wrongs those people do. Scary! The second last verse asks us to seriously consider God's words. The chapter finishes strong: *"Those who sacrifice thank offerings honor me, and to the blameless I will show my salvation"* (Psalm 50:23).

What an awesome chapter!

I could expound for hours on Psalm 50:15, which presents one of God's most awesome promises. It provided such specific encouragement for me that day. What kind of trouble? What kind of delivery? When will the delivery happen? And how?

I have learned that we don't always need to know all the particulars to rest in promises from the Word of God. God said it. I believe it. That settles it.

As I lay on the stretcher later that day, having arrived at Toronto General Hospital, the ambulance drivers kept me company as Murray dealt with paperwork. At some point, I felt anxiety rise in my chest and I again began wondering why this was happening to me.

God reminded me of His promise: *"Call on me in the day of trouble; I will deliver you, and you will honor me."*

I immediately thanked and praised Him for His Word and promises. I can honestly say that this was the last day I ever questioned why God does what He does, or allows what He allows. When He tells me to read part of the Bible for a given situation, I do it. It's comforting to know that God is interested in us, as all parents are of their children. He gives what we really need when we really need it. Trust and faith come into play, along with obedience.

The medical assessment at Toronto General Hospital redirected me to a specialist who helpfully identified certain minerals of which my body was grossly deprived. His assessment also recommended that I get daily help at home for a while. I was extremely thankful for the Red Cross's homemaking service, which provided practical assistance for five mornings every week. Within a few months, with rest and effective mineral therapy, I gradually regained some energy.

After that, my life was full, satisfying, and very busy with family responsibilities, community and church volunteer work, and children's activities like skating, baseball, hockey, kids clubs, youth meetings, school, and homework. Children certainly do bring blessings, frustrations, joy, challenges, and lots of good times.

During those years, health challenges seemed to plague me. I believe that my resilience and strength to keep going came from God.

I include a note that Debra-Kaye sent to me during one of my hospital stays. The note was delivered with beautiful flowers.

Mom, Miss Johnson gave us these flowers. I thought it seemed they were mainly for you so you should have them. It seems like every time you go away to the hospital, my eyes wet the pillow. Last night my eyes were watery. No one hears me because I don't cry out loud. I did my skirt last night, the tearing out and re-sewing. Now I will study science. I have some things to memorize.

Deb

As one can imagine, my eyes became watery as well.

During maple sugar time on the Sisson farm, everyone helped when necessary, including the older grandkids. Those on boiling duty could count on Grama Sisson's homemade treats for the sugar shack. She often had food ready when someone took a break from their shift.

My four sisters-in-law often went to the bush, but not me. I didn't have the stamina to do that kind of work, so I stayed home and looked after the younger kids, providing snacks and meals as required.

Murray's parents had fifteen grandkids. Sometimes the older ones made their way to our home, too, when they got tired, wet, or cold. We had a grand time.

The work during maple season was often accomplished by our five families working together, along with one or two hired men. We received gallons of maple syrup in exchange for our work, which suited everyone.

Murray was transferred once in his career with Ontario Hydro. With that transfer, our family relocated to the town of Napanee. We enjoyed that area for five years with a new church, new friends, new schools, and new neighbours. It was a good move for our family. Many friends from those years have remained in our lives.

A gal called Ann became my very good friend and we have been thick as thieves ever since, supporting one another through the raising of our six children. We had a lot of good times and a lot of laughs. We also supported each other through the loss of loved ones and hospital stays. We also attended church, went to church camps, took trips, and made so much tea and many homemade biscuits.

Murray was eventually transferred back to Minden and our children finished their elementary and high school years in Haliburton County.

When Ann married her husband Sandy, I was honoured to stand with her. It was a lovely wedding. Sandy was a military man, and over the years they lived in places like Alberta, Manitoba, Ontario, and Colorado Springs. No matter how many miles away they were, Ann and I remained lifetime friends. We are only a call away, or a click, or even a flight if needed. As a nurse, she has touched many lives. She's the best!

During our time in Napanee, my dad passed. He'd had a leg amputated due to a serious artery disease. The first amputation took his foot and part of his lower leg. During those weeks, I prayed for his comfort, his spiritual life, and wisdom for the medical team. I prayed that God would confirm to me that my dad had accepted Him and would be in heaven when his life on earth was done.

He endured an extreme amount of pain following that surgery and I found myself adding to my initial prayer, saying that I would be okay if God took him tomorrow. All I needed was this confirmation.

It was difficult to see him in such pain and I continued to pray the same way.

Within four weeks, a second surgery removed his leg above the knee since the artery behind the knee had continued to be an issue. This relieved a good percentage of the pain.

I continued to pray for him and the team working with him. Eventually he grew to be more comfortable with his prosthesis and made progress through rehab.

In a few months, he was discharged. Eventually he was able to accomplish some work again in his shop.

And I continued to pray for him as I had been praying.

Within two years, he was diagnosed with cancer. This involved one of his lungs and spread quickly through his bones. He only lived another two months.

My dad died on a Sunday evening while I was attending a ladies rally. Joni Erickson was the speaker. I thoroughly enjoyed Joni, but on the Saturday afternoon of the conference I just couldn't concentrate. I sat high up in the arena's bleachers and had a one-on-one time with God.

As I prayed for my dad, God spoke to me in that voice I had heard before: *"You can have assurance that your dad has received salvation."* That's all He said.

That was enough! I rejoiced.

The next day, my dad died. My brother Morley had arrived from Ecuador in time to see him, and even to feed him some soup and bread the evening before.

That weekend, my family had all been together at the hospital at various times, except me. But that was okay. I was where I needed to be. I love how God looks after the necessary details for His kids. Praise His name!

Years later, I visited the hospital in Toronto where Dad had rehab. I found the floor where he had been and sought out a nurse who had cared for him. She was a Christian and remembered him. He had inquired about her faith in God. The next morning, he had been different. She had known he'd made things right with God.

Our own family didn't escape medical challenges. We prayed for and sensed God's guidance for our children often with respect to physicians, treatments, hospital stays, and homecare. God was always close by for comfort. We accepted and appreciated help from family and friends when needed. Life went on and prayer continued to be a focal part of my life.

Our church welcomed visiting missionaries. Murray and I looked forward to meeting these families and praying for them when receiving their regular updates, praise notes, and prayer needs. It was our privilege to often provide meals in our home for missionaries and overnight accommodation when they needed it during their travels.

Our kids became very comfortable meeting these missionaries from around the world. They were interested and attentive during discussions around our table.

A man from Ireland once visited after having served in Colombia. The kids were fascinated with his Irish accent as he shared stories of his time in South America.

When he was ready to leave our home that afternoon, he reached into his pocket and gave each of our kids a dime. They looked puzzled as they accepted it.

It was Dwight who spoke up. "You shouldn't give us money. We give to missionaries."

Our missionary friend laughed. "And missionaries appreciate that, thank you. Now, every time you use a dime, you can remember to pray for a missionary."

Those impressive words taught our kids such an important lesson regarding the use of a prayer trigger.

I had opportunity to accompany Murray on one of his trips to Ecuador. We were there for ten days and travelled throughout the country. We had many adventures as we met missionaries, visited their churches, and shared their meals. We also met many locals.

One day I was scheduled to meet with one of the teachers at an Ecuadorian school. She was from England. When she discovered I could spend the day with her, she cancelled some classes, overjoyed to have another English-speaking woman to share a hot cup of tea with and have lunch. She also shared her burden of ministry. We prayed together. This was one of the highlights of the trip for me.

We also touched down in Colombia for twenty-four hours, and while there we visited missionaries, attended a delicious banquet, and saw some of the outlying areas around Bogota. What a vast and busy city! We had the privilege of viewing it from a high mountain. We had a time of prayer for the people of Columbia while up there.

Our Irish friend was back in Ireland for a brief time, so we didn't see him. We were reminded of him, though. The many stories he had shared of his work in that country brought the place to life for us.

Before returning to Canada, we spent three days in Haiti, seeing the OMS (One Mission Society) radio station, school, and guest house. We also toured other areas where the OMS missionaries worked.

A woman from our home church in Minden, Mary Lou, was a teacher with OMS during her career. What a great visit we had with her! We met so many loving Haitians.

I was thrilled to visit those countries, even though it took my body several weeks to recover upon our return. The trip stirred up my appetite for further travel. I imagined how great it would be to spend time with other missionaries in faraway countries. I so desired to see their work and become better acquainted with how and where they lived. What were their houses like? What did they eat? How were their schools and hospitals? Did they shop? What kind of sports did they enjoy? How did they relax? I wanted to visit their churches and praise God for the ministry He was doing in their lives. I continued to daydream.

Knowing that it wasn't possible for me to travel again, with my body growing weaker, I continued to partner with missionaries through the wonderful world of prayer.

On days when I needed to rest longer, I often talked to God on behalf of these missionaries. It was very rewarding to know that I could take part in their ministry through prayer.

Sometimes I would be awakened in the night with a specific missionary on my mind. I would pray as I lay in the dark, not knowing what was going on in their lives right then but knowing that it was God who had prompted me to pray. I was blessed!

Two verses come to my mind regarding praying for others and why we are to do it: *"I love the Lord, for he heard my voice; he heard my cry for mercy. Because he turned his ear to me, I will call on him as long as I live"* (Psalm 116:1–2)

Following that trip, I had the opportunity to share in churches, schools, kids clubs, and seniors groups. I so enjoyed these opportunities and felt something within me come alive as I spoke. I gave God the glory for what He was doing in the lives of so many around the world.

Little did I know that God had more trips in store for me. However, I would have to travel a very different road before any of that could unfold.

My family in 1986. Front: Phyllis, Murray, and Dwight.
Back: Donna-Lee, Dean, and Debra-Kaye.

Part Two

ONE
A Status Change

There's an old saying that tells us we're "over the hill" after turning forty. That became a reality for me. By 1985, my body was gradually falling apart.

As the year began, I noticed that store doors seemed heavier and were getting to be a bigger challenge to open. A flight of stairs was a nightmare. Muscle and joint pain were all too common. Some days, my body was too weak for me to remain standing long enough to finish preparing our evening meal. I would often slide down the side of the cupboard to sit on the floor awhile and rest.

I remember the first day the children came home from school and found me on the floor.

"Mom, what are you doing down there? Are you all right?"

It soon became a familiar sight and they stopped worrying about me leaning against something as I sat on the floor. Sometimes one of them would keep me company. We would sit together and talk about their day.

A visit to my family doctor confirmed that the late effects of polio was doing a number on my body. It's also called post-polio syndrome (PPS). More rest was required and everyone in our family helped to pick up the slack.

I discovered a nearby post-polio support group, and Murray and I attended once a month for a couple of years. These discussions were most helpful. We were all facing the challenges of this new, sometimes devastating and invasive muscle weakness, fatigue, and pain. As we met, we shared methods of coping and managing the symptoms.

Lois, one of my new friends at the support group, had contracted polio when she was fourteen, in the fall of 1949. She and her brother had grown up on a farm and both had their own cow to look after.

One morning in early September, Lois wasn't feeling well, but she wasn't quite sick enough to stay home from school. She struggled to care for her cow that morning and then made her way to school as usual. Returning home that afternoon, she felt truly unwell and asked her brother if he would look after her cow. As is often the case with siblings, he said, "No. It's your cow." She took several steps towards the barn and promptly passed out, falling to the ground.

Their doctor made a house call that evening. Following the examination, he diagnosed the dreaded polio virus. He suggested that her parents try to keep her warm. If she was still alive in the morning, they were to take her to the hospital. This was a rather brash and unsettling announcement to make as he left, but that's the way it went for that family.

The next morning, Lois was still alive. They made a quick trip to the local hospital and then had her transported to Toronto where she spent the following six months in an iron lung.

Her brother inherited the responsibility of her cow.

She survived and was eventually removed from that iron lung. In time, she recovered, and later in life she married her husband Don. She was able to have a good life, but by the 1980s she, too, had PPS. She used a scooter outside her home and clung to the support of walls and furniture when inside.

PPS hits twenty-five to forty percent of polio survivors thirty to forty years after the virus first attacks. The syndrome can present with several symptoms, for not everyone with PPS has the same ones. Some only experience one or two.

Unfortunately, I was greedy and had them all: progressive muscle and joint pain, debilitating fatigue, decreased tolerance to cold, respiratory issues, profound muscle atrophy, and swallowing challenges.

There is no cure for PPS. The only treatment is to manage the symptoms.

One evening, I tripped over Hewey, our cat. I was tripping more frequently, usually without any reason. But this time I had a reason! I went down, hurting my right foot. Hewey made a horrible howl and moved a few feet away before stopping to look back at me. Seeing me on the floor, he gave a tender meow as though to ask whether I was all right. Then he disappeared to lick his own wounds. I loved that cat.

That tumble resulted in torn ligaments in my foot. A visit to my good friend Dr. Foote the following day brought about several weeks of hydrotherapy treatment, months of wearing a removable partial cast, and the use of crutches. The ligaments mostly healed, eventually, but the strength didn't return to my leg. For the next two years, my crutches were never far away—that is, until I lost the ability to walk entirely.

The last day I drove our van in the fall of 1987, I met a truck ploughing snow on our county road. I allowed ample room for the plough and my tires went into the soft snow on the side of the road. Lacking the arm strength to steer the van back onto the road, I ended up sliding further and got stuck in the ditch.

When the driver stopped and got out of the truck, I realized that I knew him. With a grin on his face, he told me that I hadn't needed to give him that much room. He hitched up his chain and pulled our van back onto the road.

As I carefully drove on home, I knew it was time to hang up my keys. I no longer had sufficient strength to fully control the vehicle.

The weakness worsened, and a few months later I lost the ability to walk.

For the previous three years, my life and the life of our family had been gradually changing. My breathing became more laboured. Rest took over more and more of my day. Pain grew to be more prevalent. Weakness plagued every activity. Deterioration of my muscle groups continued. Enjoying a meal often resulted in choking.

I vividly remember the last day I walked. It was the last Sunday in February 1988. My morning routine was very difficult that day. I was more of a hurting unit than usual, and weaker. I got myself ready, though, and went to church with my family using my crutches for support. Sunday morning worship was always worth the extra effort.

That morning, I remained sitting during the service. Singing while sitting down was more enjoyable than trying to stand. I was thankful to be there. It was a good service and an enjoyable time visiting with people afterward.

We returned home. Climbing the three steps into our home seemed like climbing a mountain. They required almost more strength than I could muster, and afterward I went directly to my bed to rest. Debra-Kaye and Murray made lunch, and Debra-Kaye brought my food to the bed.

As I rested that afternoon, something within me knew that rest wasn't going to revive my body enough this time to get up and keep going. I cannot describe it in any other words. I know this didn't take God by surprise. He had faithfully cared for me and I knew His care would continue.

Tylenol helped the pain some and I gradually began to relax. Murray carried me to the washroom and back. I slept soundly.

The next morning, I couldn't get out of bed to stand and try to walk. After a call to our doctor, Murray drove to the hospital to borrow a wheelchair. In his mind, he was working through the reality of the situation, and by the time he arrived at the hospital he had accepted that we were now into the wheelchair season of my PPS. We had both known this was a possibility.

We were there.

A person walks until they can no longer walk. Then they sit down. That Monday morning, I began the sitting down stage of my life. The muscle weakness had moved in and taken up residence in my body. I no longer had a leg to stand on.

Very soon a homecare coordinator visited, my family doctor made house calls, and we purchased a manual wheelchair. A Red Cross support worker was provided to me and I was also visited by a physiotherapist and an occupational therapist.

Within a few months, everyone was on the same page: I indeed lacked the strength to stand and put one foot ahead of the other. Weeks of rest hadn't restored my caved-in body. And so the professionals confirmed what I already knew: I couldn't walk. They stopped pushing me to try, realizing that these efforts only further depleted the little bit of strength I had. Besides, I was making no headway in the walking department.

Once they stopped pushing, my body slowly began to relax and in time regained enough strength to be able to more comfortably bathe, dress, and feed myself. Eventually I could even sit up in my wheelchair long enough to look intelligent and carry on a conversation.

The Red Cross provided homemaking services three hours per day, five days per week. I was so appreciative of that consistent help! Two of those homemakers, Marg and Rose, became my good friends. All three of us were the same age and we had grown close to each other. Some days I spent more hours with my homemaker than with my family members. We had good times celebrating birthdays, annual Christmas lunches, and other special occasions together.

Soon more renovations had been finished, including a ramp so I could get in and out of our home with ease on my own steam. Within six months, my electric wheelchair arrived. What a great day that was! I anxiously waited for the driver to unload the machine from his van.

The technician drove it up the ramp and through the front door of our home. He then showed me everything I needed to know, and with that I began my life as a full-time electric wheelchair driver. I named the vehicle Rolls!

Rolls brought me independence. I had always enjoyed driving vehicles, including bikes, go-karts, snow machines, vans, cars, trucks, and motorcycles with my brothers. Now I drove everywhere, even to the washroom.

When my sister Joy made plans for her wedding, she asked if I would stand with her. I said I would love to… as long as she was okay that I stayed sitting. The newlyweds were married on our deck in Minden as the guests sat in folding chairs on our front lawn. She had chosen an accessible location for the wedding and delicious meal. It was a lovely day to be involved in another wedding.

As the months turned into years, Rolls transported me easily through my home, enabling me to enjoy my deck in the warmth of the summer sun and roll along with family members and friends through malls, church, and other wheelchair-accessible buildings. I could enjoy so many events with friends and family, and even carefully manoeuvre along country trails.

Rolls was my constant companion. She stood by my bed as I rested a couple times every day, patiently waiting to take me to my next destination. She balked at the sight of steps but took on the challenge of almost any incline, held open heavy store doors, and carefully weaved her way around mud puddles. She could also turn on a dime! I could have made use of a foghorn while in oblivious crowds, but that would have voided the warranty anyway.

Perhaps best of all, Rolls caught the eye of children, offering me golden opportunities to answer their questions, talk about life in the sitting position, and share Jesus along the way.

Rolls wore a magnet on her side that read "What are you and I going to do today, Lord?" This was a question I often asked as a new day dawned. That magnet also provided so many opportunities for me to share Jesus with those who showed interest.

One day as I sat in a clinic waiting room in a Toronto hospital, a patient had a question for me. He was sitting alongside Rolls, staring at that magnet. I could feel his stare.

Eventually he spoke. "Did you get religion before you went into that wheelchair or after?" I was pleased to answer, and for the next fifteen minutes we took the opportunity to visit.

Family life is different with Mom in a wheelchair. Each of our children accepted the new family dynamic in their own way. I was proud of each one and their extra measure of emotional strength. Their ages in February 1988 were twenty, nineteen, eighteen, and sixteen. I was thankful for many things during those days, especially that they weren't ten, nine, eight, and six. God had prepared us for this season of our life, and we rolled with it, praising Him for His care, comfort, protection, and blessings. On rough days, we still knew His comfort.

After our first Christmas with Mom in a wheelchair, I made an executive decision regarding our future family meals together for Christmas

Eve. I announced early in January that I was going to save loose change throughout the coming year to take our family to a restaurant.

Everyone thought that sounded like a great idea. We found a special money box and used it to deposit all our loose change. As the months passed, it began to fill with pennies, nickels, dimes, and quarters.[3] Periodically we rolled the coins and someone would exchange them for bills at the bank.

When Christmas Eve 1989 was approaching, we made a reservation. A gentle snow had begun to fall during the day of Christmas Eve and the landscape outside our home transformed into beautiful Christmas scene. The snow didn't stop us as we loaded into our van and made our way to our special dinner.

Because of the weather, we had the restaurant to ourselves. It was a quaint log-framed chalet in the country, just outside town. The warm fireplace glowed and the turkey dinner with all the trimmings was extra delicious. The staff was very attentive to our every need.

Of course, the company was the best. We were all so laidback! What a lovely time we had together. When the bill was paid, adding a generous tip, we still had some money to spare. It was a Christmas to remember. God had known we needed that special time.

---

[3] Note that this was before the advent of loonies and toonies.

TWO
Life in a Wheelchair

A power wheelchair provides mobility, brings freedom, and offers independence. I never once entertained the idea that life in a wheelchair was one of confinement.

As a wheelchair driver, I was out and about as often as I had strength to do so. I enjoyed attending Dean's baseball games in warm weather. Watching his hockey games on occasion was a highlight throughout the winter, albeit I watched from a warm part of the arena. Over the years, our children made fun of the fact that my nose immediately turned red upon entering the cold. I could have annually relieved Rudolph and led Santa's sleigh.

Our church was accessible, as well as the post office, grocery stores, and a couple of other stores in our town. However, I became aware of the many businesses and public buildings that were not. It takes very little to bring an electric wheelchair to a stop when it comes to access. They are heavy, laden with a battery and often adjustable leg riggings as well as other features necessary for the comfort of the driver.

Most manual wheelchairs can be lifted and even carried up a flight of steps, along with the occupant, but that's not the case with a power wheelchair. Turning my machine around allowed me to back over a two-inch rise, but anything higher than that left me sitting on the sidewalk looking in. On occasion, we set up eight-foot portable ramps from the van if it was imperative that I enter such a building with a couple steps, but this was seldom practical considering the space required.

I knew of at least twenty-four other people in our county who also drove wheelchairs. My concern was that I very seldom saw any of them out and about. They weren't at community events, shops, or restaurants. Nor did they attend church or visit along sidewalks to enjoy the fresh air. The disabled just didn't seem to be part of the community.

You know where this is going. I determined to encourage businesses and governments to become accessible to all and make it possible for the disabled to get out of their homes whenever possible, especially for reasons other than medical appointments and hospital stays.

My approach was to directly contact the owners of public buildings. I requested the possibility of access on behalf of all disabled persons, whether they used wheelchairs, walkers, crutches, or scooters. Even those who pushed strollers would benefit from better access.

One of my points of discussion involved the fact that disabled people face enough challenges just getting out of bed and looking after their daily needs, and sometimes they already have to rely on the care of others. They often feel like they're left out. Providing access would build confidence, provide encouragement, and remind them they are welcomed into the community. Not being able to enter shops, offices, churches, and restaurants tends to make a person feel unwelcome and isolated.

The positive response to this approach was overwhelming.

As ramps were built and renovations took place over the following year, I expressed my appreciation both in person to business owners as well as through a letter to the editor in local newspapers. That was our main source of social media in the day. These letters brought attention to my passionate concern, not only for myself but for many others in the community.

Within a few years, I started seeing other wheelchair drivers in stores, at church, at community events and sports games, out on the sidewalks, and in offices paying their own bills. It was wonderful.

A friend of mine in her eighties, Eleanor, had needed to use a scooter for some time. This dear lady had never driven a car—not even a wheelbarrow, she often said. She had difficulty understanding the concept of approaching a sidewalk curb at the proper angle, and as a result she toppled over twice. She always had a smile on her face, even when landing on the pavement. She would pick herself up, dust herself off, and keep going. She could be seen driving at the highest speed her machine would go!

One advantage of a small town is that the locals know everyone. Drivers took great care when they knew Eleanor was out doing her errands. Everyone loved this sweet lady.

One day she was speeding beside a parked car just as the driver, unaware of Eleanor, opened the door. Eleanor collided with the door and was thrown off her scooter, hurting both her and the scooter. A police officer had been in view of the accident and she lost her ride for a while.

This didn't stop her for long, though, and she continued to be as active as possible. Eleanor was one of our faithful supporters promoting access for all.

The local National Access Awareness chapter was all about access, no matter what kind or level of disability. I was privileged to be part of the movement when it began in our community. The goal was to encourage interested people to participate in conversations on creating an accessible and inclusive community.

On the national scene, National Access Awareness promoted an accessible and inclusive Canada. I was also asked to attend one of their larger-scale meetings. While there, I sat at a table with a woman who was visually impaired. Her service dog patiently sat between her chair and my wheelchair.

During the break, I drove to the refreshment table to choose my snack. When I was making my way back to my spot, my muffin perched on a serviette in my lap, I held a coffee in one hand and the machine's joystick in the other. This woman's dog kept his eye on my muffin as I approached. When I was ready to edge Rolls into my parking spot, he lunged toward my lap. As quick as you could blink, he snatched my muffin and swallowed it in one gulp.

His owner felt the jerk on the harness and suspected what had happened. When I confirmed her suspicions, I just assured her that I hadn't been hurt in any way. She then immediately disciplined her dog. So that's why he had swallowed the muffin whole! He had wanted to guarantee that his action would be worth the effort. He'd known that he would be scolded.

Revisiting that scene always brings a smile to my face.

As time passed, I was asked to represent the disabled community on a committee regarding housing in our county. It proved to be an interesting exercise, meeting new people and grasping an understanding of how such a committee works. Since the cogs of progress often move slowly, the housing project was built after we had moved on to another part of the province.

My hope is that these homes were a benefit to some of the disabled community as well as others, since this tourist area has continued to grow and develop.

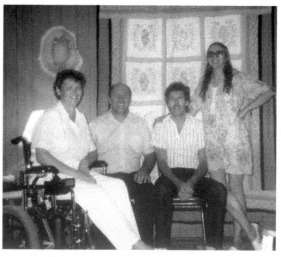

PJ and her siblings in 1989: Phyllis, Morley, Keith, and Joy.

THREE
Our Move in the Horse Trailer

The progression of PPS symptoms vary from one individual to another. The progression can be ongoing for up to five years. At the point when the muscle weakness ceases to get worse, the person stabilizes. They usually retain that level of strength until the natural aging process, or illness, causes further deterioration.

For me, it took four and a half years before I stabilized. I felt so happy when I finally realized that my body had indeed stabilized. It meant I could get on with my life as a full-time wheelchair driver, with the strength remaining to me. Over time it became clear what I could and couldn't physically accomplish.

I developed an interest in representing the Regal Gift and Card company. I also hosted a Mary Kay party, family celebrations, and other special events, as well as helping in the church. One of our local newspaper editors came to our home to interview me once, and they wrote an article on post-polio syndrome as part of an ongoing series about disabilities in the community.

While still in Minden, I had the opportunity to accompany Murray to an OMS missions conference in the United States. What a super time that was! I got to meet missionaries we knew and many new ones, as well as other supporters throughout North American. We heard the encouraging reports of God's work in so many countries.

On the Saturday evening, we listened to a music presentation from a mixed quartet from Russia. How they sang and praised our Lord! The four members were presented with a red rose as they concluded.

Following the service, the quartet stood at the front of the auditorium for any who wished to greet them—and Rolls and I were in the long lineup. When I got near the first young man, I saw his red rose fall to the floor. He didn't notice, and I decided that I could pick it up and give it to him when I got close.

He glanced to the side just as I picked up the rose and moved in to give it to him. A tear came to his eye as he thanked me profusely. I told him how blessed I had been by their ministry that evening. I so appreciated the group's musical talent and willingness to come to the United States for the conference. The people of Russia had held a sweet spot in my heart and in my prayers for many years.

Another tear rolled down his cheek as he handed me back the rose as a thank you for praying for the people of Russia.

"I can't take your rose," I said. "It was given to you!"

But he insisted, so I finally accepted the rose. It remained part of a dried flower arrangement in my home for several years, used as a prayer trigger to continue to pray for the people of Russia.

As time passed, Murray's health went south and he lost the ability to continue working. When he had to claim long-term disability, we prepared to move to a warmer part of Ontario. We intended to move to Leamington, a short drive from Point Pelee, the southernmost tip of Canada.

We contacted a real estate office and began the process of selling our home on Horseshoe Lake Road. Next, we took a scouting trip to Leamington, where we found a new home that would require only a few adjustments for wheelchair access.

After the purchase, our friends and family helped us sort, purge, and pack. Casey, a neighbour from the farm down the road, even offered to move us in his new horse trailer. Casey knew that I didn't share his acceptance of "farm smells" and he had to assure me that the trailer was indeed new!

And sure enough, it was, without a trace of farm on it. Casey was a man of his word. We were thankful for his offer and looked forward to our earthly possessions being loaded in his horse trailer.

Casey couldn't understand why Murray and I would ever want to leave our neighbourhood with such good neighbours. I tried to help him understand that the milder weather would be most beneficial with respect to our health.

When moving day arrived, it was a cool but sunny morning in late November. Several neighbours helped load the horse trailer.

While making a final tour of the empty house, Casey came inside wearing a handsome grin. "I told Murray that almost everything was loaded. There's only room for one more thing. I asked whether we should take the picnic table or you and your wheelchair. Murray suggested that I should ask you, so I'm asking."

The picnic table stayed behind.

As we arrived at Worchester Avenue in Leamington, much to our dismay, we discovered that it was not only colder than the temperature we'd left behind in Minden, but snow was coming down as well. It was very pretty, though, and rather welcoming to this northern-raised gal.

Casey made a phone call to his farm and confirmed that the sun was still shining in Minden with no sign of snow.

"So you're moving here for milder weather?" Casey said. "I can turn this rig around and take you back home."

Instead our new life began in Leamington.

FOUR

Life on Worchester Avenue

Worchester Avenue is a relatively short street, ending in a cul-de-sac. When we moved in November 1991, there were two other homes in the cul-de-sac along with ours. During our few years there, the other lots filled in with beautiful homes and good people. The neighbourhood was quite different from the country road we'd left behind, but we enjoyed our new home as well as our new neighbours.

Friends of ours from Men for Missions, an organization which Murray had been part, helped unload the horse trailer. They also provided a most welcome supper of homemade soup and freshly baked rolls with a hot cup of tea, complete with homemade pie topped with ice cream. It was delicious and warmed our bodies, while the generosity and sweet fellowship warmed our souls.

We had landed well, despite the unexpected snow and cold weather.

The snow was already melting the next morning as Casey rolled out of our neighbourhood with his empty horse trailer. This was the end of November, and a few weeks later, on Christmas Day, we watched our neighbour cut his green grass. If Casey could have witnessed the scene, his mind would have been put at ease, since he was clearing snow at his farm near Minden.

Snow never lasted long on the ground in Leamington. The milder weather did indeed prove to be a soothing balm to our bodies.

A new personal support worker joined us in our home. We also visited a few churches before settling on one to call our home church. We became acquainted with a new pharmacy, too, as well as a new doctor and various new shops. After making new friends, we quickly felt right at home.

The neighbours were very friendly, either giving a wave or coming out to have a wee visit as we went by.

A friend from down the street, Martha, often went with me for a walk-and-roll. What a blessing she was! Then there was a delightful couple from Britain who built their home just across the street from us. We all became good friends.

Ours was the only house in the cul-de-sac that left our outside light on through the night, and because of this a particular young lady felt comfortable coming to our door late one evening when she was in distress. She apologized for the lateness of the hour but explained that she'd known we would help since our house always looked so welcoming, day and night. How sweet of her to say!

The Lebanese family next door soon invited us to their home for a family barbecue, celebrating their son's baptism. The event was attended by many extended family members and we felt privileged to be part of their special day.

We also befriended an Italian family. They were very helpful when Murray was spending his last month in hospital. They had a family member on the hospital staff who was instrumental in getting Murray moved into a private room by the nursing station. She also helped me weave my way through the endless paperwork. She was my onsite advocate during that stressful time.

The newest family to build in the cul-de-sac were immigrants from Germany. We provided a meal for them the day they moved in. They were good neighbours—and when the lady of the house became ill, I was privileged to be of help to them.

We knew God had placed us in that neighbourhood for His purposes. We were blessed indeed!

Murray and I invited many people to our home as time passed. Our annual Christmas drop-in open house was a favourite occasion. These new friends all became familiar with our kitchen, making a cup of tea or coffee when they visited.

Meanwhile, I used a hands-free phone and continued to be a Regal Gift and Card consultant. Customers came to our home to pick up their orders since it was very difficult for Rolls to enter most of their homes. I also hosted a weekly study group from our church while Murray taught one in another area of town.

We enjoyed having our pastor and his wife over for lunch every month. We hosted an annual luncheon for our church's missions committee, too. We often invited friends for meals and picnics in our back yard. What great times our little home on Worchester Avenue provided for us!

A few days before we had left Minden, we brought our cat Hewey to my sister's home about ten miles north. Hewey wasn't a good traveller and we thought the long trip to Leamington wouldn't work out for either him or us. He had been born on a farm and had always lived with us in the country. We thought he wouldn't do well living in town. He loved being outside in any kind of weather. He would wander the fields and bushes and return home for supper.

My sister Joy had cats, so she was happy to take Hewey into her home. As it turned out, the day he arrived he chose to not go inside. Rather, he disappeared into the woods behind her home. She searched and searched for days but couldn't find him. Joy suspected he was trying to find his way back home. Winter was settling in, and she feared he may never be seen alive again. Possibly he had turned out to be a wolf's lunch one day.

Within five weeks of Hewey disappearing, one of Joy's neighbours called to say that a cat had come out of the woods near her home. Sure enough, the stray cat was Hewey. Joy brought him home and carried him inside. He had obviously fended for himself for those five weeks and survived. His nose appeared to have frostbite and he had lost a lot of weight, dragging his hindquarters. Hewey had been a healthy and robust large cat, with six toes on each of his front paws; he was what's known as a polydactyl cat. These cats, considered to be lucky, were extremely versatile in catching mice. No doubt those characteristics had served him well while lost in the woods.

Now he needed to be cared for, however, and Joy was just the one for the task. Within a month, she had nursed him back to health and was convinced he would be more content with Murray and me. Her three cats had their own routine. They had been sympathetic and tolerated Hewey in his weakness, but they had no intention of letting this stray cat stay with them permanently.

Dean and Donna-Lee made the trip to Leamington to bring Hewey to us. Apparently he whimpered all the way down for the five-hour trip. When he arrived, he gingerly circled each of the rooms on our main floor, sniffed the furniture, visited the kitty litter, and had a snack and a drink of water. He then found a comfortable place to sleep and was in kitty la-la-land for the next twelve hours.

He settled in quickly, and within a few days we introduced him to our back yard, which I'm sure he thought was small but safe. The other cats in the neighbourhood soon discovered there was a new cat in the cul-de-sac. Hewey was healthy and strong again and proudly protected his new property in typical cat-fashion.

Like Murray and me, Hewey was happy on Worchester Avenue.

FIVE
Living in Leamington

Colasanti's Tropical Gardens became a favourite place of ours to visit. It was open throughout the year, catering to field trips and groups with mini-golf, markets, exotic plants, crafts, and workshops, as well as a restaurant, garden centre, arcade, and petting farm. They were known for their broasted chicken and customers drove from miles away to order it. This was a beautiful place to wander and roll about with total wheelchair access.

Point Pelee National Park was another drawing card. Although the smallest national park in the country, it was a great spot for cycling, paddling, hiking, and bird-watching—all, while in a wheelchair, of course. Murray and I only had to drive thirty minutes to enjoy these amenities and we often took visiting friends and family. It was a delight.

Another local attraction was the Jack Miner Migratory Bird Sanctuary, once rated the second greatest tourist attraction in Canada. It includes a historic house, museum, cabin, nature stadium, and learning centre. We could go down the trails and feed the birds that passed through in search of food, water, and shelter. We visited at least twice a year when the fields were completely covered with birds. How did they know this place even existed? God's design for creation is amazing.

The town itself had a huge red tomato where people could take photos. The reason is that Leamington had been home to a large ketchup factory for more than a hundred years, although it closed in 2014. That was a sad year for the community. When we lived there, the smell of bubbling ketchup often filled the air and we saw tractors tow long trailers of ripened tomatoes over the country roads at harvest time.

One of our neighbours on Worchester Avenue worked at a tomato farm and frequently shared fresh produce with us that wasn't suitable for canning. This was one of the many perks of living in Leamington!

And then there was our home church. The week following our first visit, the church installed a ramp to cover the two-inch rise at the front entrance. On Sunday, teenage boys took turns unloading my wheelchair as soon as Murray pulled up—and after the service, they lingered at the door, hoping to be the one to load my chair back into the van. It was a good character-building opportunity for these young men and Murray appreciated their help.

The pastor looked beyond my wheelchair, observed my intelligence, and soon invited me to teach a Sunday school class for those in first and second grades. What a delight this was! For my assistant, they assigned a young woman who was interested in learning how to teach. She served as my arms and legs since these young ones were an ambitious lot. Within a year, she took over that class and I was asked to serve as the Sunday school superintendent. This, too, was a privilege.

Murray and I enjoyed being a part of various groups in the church and community. Since he was retired and I was disabled, we also qualified to join the seniors ministry, even though we were both younger than most of the others who attended these activities.

When I became familiar with the town, I ventured off one day to the shopping mall on my own. The weather was clear and the temperature perfect for a late spring day. So off I rolled! I arrived in about a half-hour and thoroughly enjoyed my time at the mall.

Soon I began my roll back home. Just moments past four o'clock in the afternoon, I came to the busy multilane intersection by the ketchup factory. Crossing here turned out to be more of a challenge than I had anticipated. It was shift-changing time and I should have known better. I scolded myself for not leaving the mall somewhat sooner.

I started out on the green "walking" light, but I needed a lot of time to get off the sidewalk and onto the street. I also sensed that the driver planning to make his right-hand turn was extremely anxious.

He no doubt wished I had stayed home where he maybe thought I belonged.

Fearing that I wouldn't have enough time to complete the long crossing, I decided right away to go back to the sidewalk. Good decision. I drove onto the sidewalk just as that impatient driver made his turn, revving by me. My heart raced.

Another driver who had been approaching the intersection had witnessed my dilemma. As the "walking" light turned green again, this driver turned on his flashers, got out of his vehicle, took his own life in his hands, and manually stopped traffic, motioning for me to cross. I started rolling and gave a wave of appreciation to him.

All lanes of the traffic came to a stop until I was safely on the other side. My heart raced again, this time with a mix of fear and excitement. How grateful I was for that gentleman! Perhaps he was a person of authority, off-duty. I trust he will receive his reward in heaven.

This proved to be rather an unsettling adventure, though, and I never travelled to that mall again by myself.

I enjoyed many other adventures while rolling out on my own in Leamington. I always remembered to sufficiently charge the wheelchair battery before leaving home. These ventures included traveling to a convenience store, hair salon, pharmacy, chiropractic clinic, and coffee shop. I also visited all the nearby neighbourhoods as often as I was able. The fresh air, whether brisk or warm, invigorated me. This town had quite advanced wheelchair accessibility compared to Minden, for which I was grateful. This fact alone had made the move worthwhile.

In August 1993, our church held a week of evening children's meetings. Many kids showed up on the Monday evening and we all had such a fun time with games, singing, and crafts. The gospel message was shared by a children's camp director from the area. A young girl then indicated that she wanted to ask Jesus into her life, and I was asked to talk with her. In speaking with her only a few minutes, I realized that she had indeed understood the salvation message. The opportunity was mine to hear her pray to accept Jesus into her young life.

Upon returning home, there was a message on our phone from my nephew Brian, who was attending university in Texas. Brian was the eldest of my brother Morley's three sons. In the voicemail, he simply asked that someone return his call.

Donna-Lee did that and received the news that his dad had died that day in Ecuador from a sudden heart attack. What? We'd had no idea that Morley had been having health issues!

Donna-Lee was in shock and in tears as she relayed the message to us.

We needed to get the news to Mom and my siblings. Both Murray and Donna-Lee agreed the calls should be made but couldn't bring themselves to do so, so Rolls and I headed down the hall to the office from the living room where we'd been sitting and trying to absorb the news.

PJ and Murray in 1994.

I made the calls. It wasn't easy. When I spoke with my brother Keith, we both agreed he should tell Mom together. He and Bernice picked up our sister Joy, so she would be there, too. I also called some aunts and uncles who would pass on the news to other family and friends.

It's interesting how the cycle of the spiritual keeps turning. The early part of the evening had been filled with rejoicing for the young girl who'd found her way to God. All this while my brother was leaving this world and entering his heavenly home.

Morley had always said that if he passed in Ecuador, his wish was to be buried there. Both he and Darlene were well respected where they had lived and served the people of Ecuador for twenty-five years. Their town provided a burial place, and all the nearby shops closed for the funeral.

Morley was fifty-one years old when he finished his earthly journey. Too young to die, many said.

Following his funeral, eight young Ecuadorian men gave their lives to Jesus. It would be interesting to know what they have done with their lives in the past thirty-some years.

SIX

The Miracle on Worchester Avenue

February 20, 1995 was a Monday... and a great day for a miracle. The morning passed as any morning for a wheelchair driver should go. I got up and had breakfast before the homemaker arrived. Then I showered and dressed before she and I had our coffee break together. Following my morning rest, I made a few phone calls at my desk. Murray and I then had lunch. Afterward he had his usual snooze on the sofa while watching the TV news. I had my afternoon rest, and then Murray drove me to the mall. A few purchases and interactions with friends made for a delightful excursion and soon we returned home.

Donna-Lee was living with us at the time while on staff at our church. She and Murray both had a meeting at the church that evening, so off they went after we had supper together.

Around seven o'clock, I was preparing for an early bedtime. My day had been full and tiring. While driving my wheelchair up to our washroom vanity, I suddenly felt a complete absence of pain, weakness, and discomfort. Wow!

Pain is an interesting part of life. As in my case, I believe a person can grow accustomed to pain while learning how to cope and trying to ignore it, to the extent that one can become almost oblivious to the unwelcome sensation.

However, in that split second I sensed the pain completely leave me. It was such a strong sensation that I decided to reverse Rolls and stand up.

Even while standing, I felt no pain but rather a feeling of total wellness.

I remained standing and still felt no pain. I didn't fall. In the previous seven years, I had come to appreciate just how long thirty seconds can be. If I tried to stay on my feet longer than thirty seconds while dressing or transferring from one place to another, debilitating pain would shoot up my legs through my back and I would pass out.

No such feeling followed today.

Discomfort, weakness, and pain were all I had known for years. I couldn't remember feeling well and strong as a young girl before polio.

Immediately I knew that God had healed me and I began thanking and praising Him.

Right away, I decided to clean. I love to clean and had watched homemakers, family, and friends clean my home for seven years.

I squatted down, feeling strong. No pain! I retrieved the cleaning supplies from under the basin, stood up comfortably, and began cleaning to my heart's delight, praising God as I worked. I was working. Wow!

My bathroom wasn't in need of much by way of cleaning since our homemaker had been in that morning, but what a delight it was for me to go over everything at the vanity and put a fresh shine on it. I didn't move my feet; I just stood and cleaned.

Then I heard God speak: *"Would you be willing to share with others what I am doing in your life?"*

I said yes! That's when I knew that I could do more than stand, bend, squat, reach, and clean. I could walk!

I reversed Rolls further out of the way. Ours was a large bathroom, since I needed a five-foot radius to turn my rig around. There was room for me to walk around. I even did a few exercises, reaching up with my arms, then bending down to touch my toes. What a great time I had as I praised God!

Now what should I do? I asked myself.

I knew Murray and Donna-Lee wouldn't be home until nine-thirty or later, so I walked through our home. Everything, including the furniture and view out the windows, looked so different from a standing position. What a wonderful time I had!

This was so unexpected. I had never once asked God to heal me. I had always left such things up to Him, knowing that if He chose to heal me, that would be great; if not, His grace was sufficient. I know that may sound rather trite, but that's the way I thought. Who was I to try to tell God exactly what He should do with my life anyway? He was the designer of my life… of all our lives. We are His business. Our business is to be faithful to Him with the life He gives. His Word says so, and I believe it.

It's impossible to comprehend just how those moments felt on February 20, 1995, unless you've experienced something similar. As I write this in the fall of 2023, I still feel shivers running up and down my spine. That evening, I basked in God's lively and lovely presence. I wanted to savour the moment, yet I felt compelled to be active and do something.

No one had ever been interested in tidying the top shelf in one of the closets of our large bedroom, so I decided to do it. I couldn't find a footstool, so I picked up a chair from the kitchen—this felt so good—and carried it down the hallway and into the bedroom. I placed it beside the open closet door, climbed up, and got to work.

What fun I had! It probably took an hour to discover what was all being kept on that shelf, then sort and rearrange it all. I moved a few items to other closets or areas of the home. At the end, I was pleased with my work. How great it was to be able to do such work after God had put me back on my feet after seven years in the sitting position.

I had worked up an appetite by this time, so I made myself a snack and delicious hot cup of tea. I sat at the table on a kitchen chair and enjoyed it to the fullest. I then went to bed.

What a great Monday on Worchester Avenue!

How should I tell Murray? I wondered. *Should I tell him, or just show him? When should I do this?*

As I lay in bed, asking God to help me to figure out how and when to do it, I felt that I should keep it to myself until the morning. I still wanted to bask in this unbelievable and wonderful event, contrary though it was to the scientific law that I should never walk again.

A few people later commented that I probably hadn't known whether I would still be able to walk the next morning, but that wasn't the case at all. I knew God had brought about this wonderful event. It was for real and had been accomplished for His reasons. This was not a fleeting happening.

It wasn't unusual for me to be asleep when Murray returned from an evening meeting. He later told me that he did notice that my feet weren't cold.

Being tired himself, he went off to sleep.

I woke early the next morning but waited until Murray was up and went into the bathroom. While he shaved, I decided to get in my wheelchair and park in the hallway, then get out of my wheelchair and walk behind him to the laundry area at the end of the bathroom.

As I walked behind him, looking at him in the mirror, I said, "Oh, by the way, Murray, I can walk."

He stopped shaving and looked up to the mirror. "Wow!"

I reached to open the door of the laundry closet. I cannot tell you how the next few minutes went. It was a private moment between us.

What a great breakfast we had that morning. When Donna-Lee came upstairs from her area in the basement, I greeted her in the kitchen, still sitting in my wheelchair, since I didn't want to shock her without any warning. She started to pour her orange juice.

"Donna-Lee, I have great news," I said. "I can walk."

I proceeded to reverse Rolls, stand, and walk to the living room. She became very excited, telling me to stop and sit down before I fell. She couldn't believe what she was seeing.

As the three of us rejoiced that day, we discussed how we should tell people. One thing I didn't want to do was shock anyone, or possibly cause someone a heart attack. As you can imagine, it was shocking indeed!

We made phone calls to family members in the Minden area, as well as friends who lived a distance away. Dwight, Debra-Kaye, and Dean all made arrangements to travel to Leamington for the weekend to see and celebrate.

We kept the miracle lowkey the rest of the day as we adjusted to the fact that a disabled person no longer lived in this home on Worchester

Avenue. I rejoiced as I worked in the kitchen, looked after the laundry, and moved about our home as an abled body person.

I went out on the deck at the back of our home and looked at the long ramp our friend Stewart had built for me to access the yard. However, today I used the three steps. I was like a kid with a new toy, walking down the steps, then turning around and walking back up the steps. I also walked downstairs to the basement to see how things looked there, then walked back up. Can you possibly imagine how great this felt?

Part Three

ONE

Immediately After a Miracle

When reading my Bible as a young teenager, I felt intrigued by the many wonderful events as Jesus walked the earth as recorded in the New Testament, including His physical healings, changing water into wine, feeding thousands of people with a little boy's lunch, raising Lazarus from the grave, calming violent storms, and catching fish where professional fishermen had scoured the waters and found none. So many people were healed in various ways.

Anyone who had witnessed or been personally touched by a miracle of Jesus must have gone on to lead a different life. How could they not have! I was always curious as to what happened to these people afterward.

Mark 1:40–45 tells of the man who was immediately healed of leprosy. We read that Jesus moved with compassion toward this man. The man's life was drastically changed.

Mark 2:1–12 then tells of another man immediately healed from paralysis. I know his life would have been so very different.

In Mark 8:22–25, we read of a blind man who was healed. I can't identify with blindness, but I suspect becoming fully sighted must have been a huge change.

Mark 9:14–29 tells of a boy with an evil spirit. He, too, was healed. That not only would have given him a normal, wholesome life, but also his family.

In John 5:1–14, an invalid was instantly healed by Jesus.

What wonderful miracles these were! And so many more are recorded in Scripture. These miracles would have changed these people's lives indeed. Scripture does tell us that most were thankful and praised Jesus as they went out and told others.

I know two facts from experience. First, life is very different following a miracle. Second, God does not waste a miracle.

TWO
A Packed Week

On Wednesday, our pastor and his wife, Bob and Eleanor, were scheduled to come over for our monthly lunch together. We decided they should be the first to be informed in Leamington.

That morning, I prepared a roast beef dinner rather than the usual soup and sandwiches or barbequed burgers and salad which either my homemaker, Murray. or Donna-Lee would prepare. This meal was going to be a celebration!

I met them at the door—in Rolls, since I didn't want to shock them immediately on an empty stomach. Donna-Lee then placed the bowls of food and plate of meat on the table.

Our pastor smiled. "Oh Donna-Lee, you have outdone yourself today."

No one made a comment. We all just smiled as we sat down at the table.

As we finished the first course, I told them that we had a surprise for them. They began guessing what it might be. There was laughter in their attempts to discover the surprise.

Finally, our Pastor made a joke: "You're going to tell us you can walk."

"You guessed it," I said. "I'll show you."

I reversed Rolls and parked her out of the way. Then I stood to my feet, picked up the plate of cookies, and started to walk toward the living room.

Silence!

I looked in their direction. "We'll have coffee and cookies in the living room."

As I placed the plate of cookies on the coffee table, I turned to glance back to the kitchen. Bob and Eleanor were sitting at the table with their mouths ajar. Murray and Donna-Lee had stayed with them, I suspect to prop them up in the event they were to keel over.

They slowly came from the kitchen, wondering if it was okay to give me a hug. Then the questions began. After answering, we started praising God. I'm not sure if we ever did enjoy the cookies with coffee.

We had another hour of fellowship, ending with all five of us standing in a circle for prayer in the middle of our living room.

"Will you give your testimony at church this Sunday?" Bob asked as they walked to the door to leave. "I'll be in touch."

That evening, my small group met in our home for Bible study as usual. How was I to reveal the miracle to them? I decided to bring Rolls back out and met them at the door. We had a good study, followed by our time of sharing praise notes and prayer requests.

At the appropriate time, I chose to give my praise note.

They were shocked and wanted to see me walk, so I parked Rolls out of the way again. She was getting used to being parked out of the way; I could almost hear her say, "Well, if I'm not needed…"

I walked about and stood as I answered the many questions. Our friend Dan said that he had known I must have something special to share that evening since I'd had a different look on my face. He had noticed it when he first arrived, although he hadn't known what the news would be. He had suspected it was something good.

What a special time of fellowship we had. Over the past few years, we had shared often, rejoicing as well as shedding tears, praying for one another and others, even for people we didn't know personally. Now we were also able to share in this obvious miracle of God.

We parked Rolls in a strategic spot in the living room, standing proud. She had served me well and was eventually moved to the home of a woman in our area who had muscular scoliosis. My manual wheelchair went to a friend in Minden who needed some extra assistance.

On Thursday morning, I called Martha, my good friend on Worchester Avenue who often accompanied me for our neighbourhood walk-and-roll. I also called another good friend, Grace, among other friends.

When Martha heard the news, she responded in a high-pitched tone of excitement. "Don't go anywhere! I'll be right there."

She must have run down the street, because very soon she was ringing our doorbell. I was standing as I opened the door. She reached out for a huge hug.

"Oh, you are much taller than I expected!" she said.

What fun we had.

Grace arrived within minutes. Lots of tea and sweets were served that day as others filtered through our door. There were many tears of joy, questions, and laughter as we chatted and praised God for this awesome event. Praise was the agenda for that day, and for many more to come.

On Friday, we called a few more people to share the news. We received a variety of responses, as was the case over the following weeks and months, even years. Most rejoiced. Some were sceptical. We accepted all responses.

Another call I made was for an appointment with my doctor. It was time for my six-month checkup, so the appointment was made for Monday. I didn't share my news with the receptionist on the phone.

On Friday evening, our kids arrived. What fun! We enjoyed a wonderful Saturday together. It was unlike any other Saturday our family had ever spent together.

I suddenly found myself needing shoes. During the seven years in my wheelchair, I had worn inexpensive canvas summer shoes to cover my feet. I had several pairs in pretty colours to match outfits, and they were roomy enough to be comfortable. But muscle atrophy over the years hadn't been a friend to my body, especially my right leg and foot, which had never developed properly. My close friends were allowed to call it a funny little foot.

Through the miracle, God straightened out my foot and placed some flesh and muscle on it. A bit of deformity was left, but that didn't matter to me. It was His business, and He had completely fixed all the other areas of my body.

However, the deformity did allow me to share the story with shoe salespeople. Over the years, curious shoe clerks asked whether I would mind talking about the unusual nature of my misshapen foot.

That Saturday, I was delighted to share my story. I bought a pair of running shoes and a pair of dress shoes that day. This would be the first of many, many shoe salespeople having the opportunity to hear my story in the coming years.

I also bought a purse. Living in a wheelchair doesn't lend itself to carrying a traditional purse, so I had used a pouch for necessary items. It had been attached to Rolls, and always kept within reach.

On our Saturday together, we went shopping and even walked into Tim Hortons for a coffee. We later shared a meal together at home.

Then came Sunday.

There were basically three categories of people: those we called, those who heard the news through the grapevine, and those who still hadn't heard. When I shared my testimony, there was rejoicing, scepticism, questions, and praising. Some wondered who this woman was who walked around with my husband. Some kept their distance. Some asked if they could hug me. still others didn't ask; they just leaned in for the hug. It was a blessed time indeed.

One man told me that if I was still walking in three months, he would believe it was a miracle.

"I can't believe I actually said that," he told me when I encountered him twenty-seven years later. "I am so sorry."

A mother arrived at church with her two school-aged children. This was their third week coming to church, and we had met them in the fellowship hall the first two Sundays when she brought her children to the Sunday school. This Sunday, she arrived a bit early and we saw each other in the entryway. She wanted to share something with me about her children, so we talked for a few minutes with no one else around. She then took her children into the fellowship hall.

I had been asked to share briefly with the adult Sunday school class that morning regarding the miracle. While I spoke, the young mother listened intently. I shared the highlights of the story and answered some questions, all the while giving God the glory for what He was doing in my life.

I returned to the fellowship hall just before the kids classes were finished. That's when this young mother raced into the hall behind me, saying that she had hardly been able to wait for the class to be over to talk with me.

I smile every time I think of this conversation. She was bubbling over and could hardly talk.

"I thought there was something different about you when we spoke in the entryway," she said to me. "I wondered if you had been wearing glasses last week!"

"No," I replied. "I was wearing a wheelchair."

We both laughed.

There were of course many questions from the kids, as they noticed right away that I was standing in front of them and walking about. One little fellow raised his hand and was anxious to tell me that I had forgotten to bring my wheelchair. He was seriously concerned.

As God would have it, this was the thirteenth Sunday of the thirteen-week sessions we had been teaching on the subject of miracles in the Bible. The thirteenth class was an overview of twelve different miracles that had been discussed during those weeks.

The teachers and students went to their respective classes, and the teachers later reported to me what a special time of discussion they'd had in their classes that day. Witnessing a modern-day miracle appeared to have been a bonus.

Only God could arrange the timing of such a day.

The morning worship service followed at 11:00 a.m. and closed with the song "In His Time." Our pastor then called me up: "Phyllis Sisson is going to come to the platform now to share her testimony."

An uncanny buzz went through the crowd of about one hundred twenty-five people. Many still hadn't heard of the miracle or yet seen me that morning. People knew the platform wasn't wheelchair accessible, so they must have wondered how I would get onto the platform.

As I stood to my feet and moved into the aisle, a unified gasp arose from the congregation. What a wonderful experience this was to walk up the aisle and ascend those few steps onto the platform, not needing to hold onto the railing.

I shared the exciting update of what God had been doing the past week, giving God the glory.

That evening, a film was shown in our church. It had been scheduled several months in advance. Words cannot express how I felt sitting with the church, filled to the brim with people, watching "Jesus," a film depicting the ministry of Jesus, including many of the physical miracles He performed while in the world.

We had invited the British couple from our cul-de-sac and they'd travelled with us to the evening service. What a special opportunity this was to hear their comments and questions after the film. We finished the evening with them in our home for tea and sweets.

Monday morning came, marking the one-week anniversary of the miracle. A few inches of snow had fallen overnight and Murray drove me to my follow-up appointment in our daughter's car. How great it was to walk to the car and just get in and be ready to go. As a full-time wheelchair driver, we had always needed to allow extra time to load me and Rolls into our van.

When we arrived at the clinic, our doctor was clearing snow off the ramp. Murray parked beyond the ramp, and then we proceeded to walk up it, saying good morning to our doctor. He stopped shovelling and gave us room to walk by. He didn't recognize either of us, since he had never seen me walking before.

We chose to wait until he came inside to say anything.

When the receptionist and nurse saw me walking in, though, the questions began. The doctor came in through a back door and didn't hear this chatter. The nurse showed me to the examination room as usual.

The doctor then came into the room with a shocked expression on his face. He looked at my file, looked at me, then looked back at the file. He did this three times before he spoke.

"Phyllis, where is your wheelchair?" he said with a cautious but professional calm.

It was priceless!

I talked. He listened. He then asked a few questions, and I answered. He performed the usual six-month muscle strength test, meant to determine whether there had been further noticeable deterioration. He couldn't believe what he was witnessing.

He had more questions, and eventually he asked whether I would mind him calling another doctor to the clinic to see me.

Sure, I had no problem with that.

That doctor and I had never personally met. He had, however, heard of my disability.

After hearing my answers to his five questions, he turned to my doctor. "We can't touch this. We have a miracle on our hands!"

They both stood around in shock, but neither of them had anything more to say other than "Enjoy your new life." They wore satisfying and still somewhat questionable expressions.

My doctor had always reminded me to call the office in about five months to schedule the next six-month appointment. That morning, he did not.

As I walked out of the exam room, there was a buzz. The news had spread to every patient coming and going. Murray had fielded as many questions as possible while I was with the doctors. The nurse and receptionist were both aglow. They had never witnessed such a wonderful happening. It made their day!

I soon attended my previously scheduled chiropractic appointment. A monthly treatment during my wheelchair years had provided some bodily comfort, albeit temporary. I expected the chiropractor to witness how different my body was, especially my back, giving even more credence to the miraculous healing.

He was shocked when he saw me walking, but he refused to check anything. I asked whether he would just run his skilled hands down my spine, as he usually did to determine areas of need. He would not. He had no idea what could have happened to me in the previous week, but he didn't believe it would hold and didn't want to be accused of having any part in it.

I was surprised by his response, but I respected it.

"If you're still walking in a month's time," he added, "you had better come in for a treatment because you will surely need it."

He watched me walk out of his room. His look of dismay was evident. I couldn't help but feel badly for him.

Checking with the receptionist on my way out, I verified that my name was on the appointment schedule for a four-week checkup.

When I returned a month later, the chiropractor mentioned that he had read something about "the miracle lady" in the local newspaper. He didn't want to talk further about the article, though. He checked my back and couldn't find anything that needed attention. He hesitantly acknowledged that my body had been obviously changed. The only thing wrong were signs of the beginning of a sore throat. He suggested that I see my doctor for treatment.

He tried to smile. "I wouldn't want to read in the newspaper next week that the miracle lady of Leamington had died of a throat infection."

He still seemed sceptical, puzzled, and confused as to what could have happened in my body to produce such a drastic change, but it seemed to be holding. Those were his words.

I wasn't in need of any further chiropractic treatments for several years, until a shoulder injury from a slip in the bathtub needed attention. By then I was living elsewhere and received help from a different chiropractor.

The reaction of my chiropractor in Leamington is one of many I observed in the months and years to follow. Most people accepted the story and praised God for His awesome ways. Many have been encouraged to believe in God. For others, hearing my testimony strengthened their faith.

Two people had suspected I probably could have walked all along and had only pretended to be disabled. Ouch! A few said that they would only believe it was a miracle if they could have witnessed it.

Some remained sceptical. The miracle was an unbelievable event.

No matter the reactions, God asked me to share with others what He was doing in my life, so I purposefully continue to do so. Praise His name!

THREE
1995

Word of the miracle on Worchester Avenue spread rapidly. Our phone began ringing. Calls came from perfect strangers. One such stranger then knocked on our door within an hour to see that I was really walking. Beatty and Barb, directors of Men for Missons, called from abroad to rejoice with us. Local newspapers called for interviews, as well as a radio station. We were invited to Catholic schools for show-and-tell during their studies on miracles. We spoke to a variety of groups and gatherings, the ages of these groups ranging from children to seniors.

Initially, neighbours wondered who that lady was on Worchester Avenue who looked like me. One neighbour thought I must have a twin sister visiting.

What exciting times we had in the following weeks! My time seemed to be made up of a lot of standing around, walking about, and talking. What a treat it was to get up off a chair and walk with no part of my body hurting. I praised God regularly.

I renewed my driver's license and we traded our van for a car. I bought a pair of casual shoes. We made a trip to Minden to visit family and friends. The local newspaper there wanted an interview, printing the story.

Murray and I especially enjoyed the next few months. We felt like a new couple with a special lease on life. His health seemed to be in a level state, too, and so we enjoyed taking daytrips. We took a few holidays, often visited friends and family, and attended a variety of barbeques. We treated ourselves for breakfasts out, as well as lots of picnics in the pleasant weather. A young couple in our church asked if I would be the organist for their wedding. We were privileged to participate in another wedding!

One early summer day, I participated in a fundraiser walkathon for the Pregnancy Crisis Centre. The five-kilometre walk took place in one of the delightful conservation areas in Leamington. This was not a race, just a walk.

Several dozen walkers arrived that bright sunny morning, and we were off. There were enthusiasts garbed in proper walking attire, others in casual jeans or shorts, and a few young mothers with babies in strollers. Others were well on in years but in good shape for the walk.

I so enjoyed the walk, stopping at the checkpoints for a drink of water and chatting with volunteers. I talked with other walkers as I moved along. I praised God for the ability to participate. Many friends and family had generously supported me and I was thrilled to add to the overall funds raised.

A local newspaper reporter was on deck as we arrived back to our starting point, wishing to interview the first three people to finish the walk, of which I was one. It was such a fulfilling and amazing morning for me, another fun event in this new life God had provided.

As the summer of '95 progressed, Murray started to slow down. Four years previously, he had been diagnosed with a liver disorder and the effects were becoming evident. By August, he was not as well, but he kept going as much as possible. He had started a renovation project in our basement and worked when he was able. He struggled but continued with his usual activities in the community and at church.

In October, a part-time secretary position opened at the church. Murray strongly suggested that I apply, but I had second thoughts since he was requiring more help at home. I didn't like leaving him alone too long. Even so, he felt I should take the opportunity to join the workforce.

I applied and was accepted. This position was the equivalent of three days a week with several hours being flexible. This worked for us.

During my teenage years, I had shown an interest in secretarial work. My parents had recognized this and allowed me to be responsible for a good portion of their business's office work. Upon graduation from high school, I worked for a year in Toronto in a secretarial position for a finance company. Office work was always welcome in my life. While raising children, I had often volunteered for groups in the community, doing secretarial work for church and community.

And as of October 1995, I was back in the office chair and immensely enjoying the work and interaction with people.

Our daughter Debra-Kaye married her husband Andrew that same month in a lovely wedding. We were pleased that Murray was well enough to attend, walk our bride down the aisle, and make a wonderful speech at the reception. As he walked from the platform, Debra-Kaye met him. A beautiful picture was snapped of the two of them, trickles of tears moistening their cheeks. It was precious!

The busyness of the Christmas season was indeed special for me that year as a walking person. By late November, our home was decorated. It had been a challenge to convince Murray it would be permissible to erect an artificial Christmas tree that year since he wasn't well enough to undertake our usual traditions.

Since we had married in 1966, one of our traditions had been to find the perfect tree in the woods, chop it down, and bring it home. It was often laden with snow. This tradition had started on his parents' farm near Minden.

For our first Christmas together in 1966, in our winterized country cottage, our cat Pete went with us to Murray's dad's bush and found the sweetest little tree. Our living room wasn't very big, but that little tree was just perfect.

As soon as they were big enough to keep up with their dad, clad in warm snowsuits and boots, our children always looked forward to the Christmas tree adventure. When we weren't in the area anymore, we were either invited to a friend's farm or visited a tree farm for the annual tradition of finding the perfect tree.

In 1995, we found the perfect artificial tree in a store, purchased it, and had it decorated by the end of November. Our shopping wasn't finished yet, though, nor were the Christmas sweets made, menus in place, or groceries purchased. But there would be time for all that amidst the busyness of December.

Or so I thought.

Murray's health seemed to worsen throughout the autumn with more discomfort daily. His energy level dropped significantly, and a consult with our doctor didn't bring any comfort.

By the second week of December, our Christmas preparations were still on the to-do list.

The evening of December 13 was a rainy one. I had been asked to speak at a ladies Christmas event in Leamington. What a great time that was, enjoying the fellowship with these ladies as we celebrated Jesus being the reason for the season.

Bill, a friend of Murray's, came to our home to spend the evening with him. When I returned prior to ten o'clock, he told me that Murray hadn't been feeling well as the evening progressed and had gone to bed a half-hour previously. Murray had appeared to be sleeping when Bill last checked him.

Before going home, which was also in the neighbourhood, Bill reminded me to call if I needed either he or his wife Elaine for anything. What great friends they were!

As I went into the bedroom, Murray stirred and I could tell he was terribly uncomfortable. I turned on a lamp and saw that his skin was more jaundiced than it had been the previous few years. He was in pain and quickly becoming feverish. I had been told four years ago, while Murray was under the care of a Toronto liver clinic, to watch for these very symptoms. If they appeared, he would need to get to the ER pronto. The warning was that this turn of events could take his life quickly, maybe even before he could get to a hospital.

I immediately called for an ambulance. I also called Elaine and asked if I could pick her up in my car on the way to the hospital. I felt like I may need someone with me.

Murray's vitals were awry and the attending doctor said his condition was life-threatening. She suspected his liver was shutting down.

Murray caught my eye with a slight smile through his pain. We had made it through the first hurdle; he was still alive when he arrived at the hospital. I returned the smile. Murray was prepared to leave this world if it was his time. We prayed, thanking God for His presence, committing this time to God, and praying for the nurses and doctors and that Murray would be a blessing.

Within the hour, Murray was admitted and settled into a room. I was told that if he made it through the night, arrangements would be made to have him transferred to a London hospital. By then, he was medicated and sleeping. I was advised to go home and get some rest in preparation for the next day. The staff assured me he would be well cared for and I would receive a phone call if necessary.

As Elaine and I walked out of the hospital, we were greeted by icy rain. We both set to the task of clearing the freezing rain from my car windows as we talked. Elaine felt that the seriousness of Murray's current health issue wasn't registering with me. I assured her that we had been living with this very possibility for the past four years. In fact, four years ago he had been given about two years to live. As a result, he was already on borrowed time. So we had talked it through and given Murray's health to God during those first few weeks when he had been diagnosed with ascending cholangitis of the liver.

When I dropped Elaine off at her home, she seemed satisfied that I was indeed aware of the seriousness of Murray's condition. She prayed that I would get some sleep that night.

Once home, I made several calls, first to our children and then a few family members and our pastor. I intentionally contacted people to pray and asked if they would pass on the request to their respective prayer groups across Canada and to our many friends abroad.

I made a hot cup of tea to go with a wee snack, and I got into bed by 1:00 a.m. I had done all that was necessary and was blessed with several hours of solid sleep.

Upon arriving at the hospital the next morning, I learned that Murray's vitals were stable and he had slept. Arrangements were made for his transfer.

Thus, his hospital journey began.

Over the following eleven days, tests were performed and further diagnoses made. The bowel was scattered with cancer and his liver was in failure. He wasn't expected to live long. However, he was stable enough to come home for Christmas.

We arrived by 5:00 p.m. on Christmas Eve and were strongly advised to call an ambulance should anything change.

The Christmas shopping wasn't finished, the Christmas goodies not yet baked, and food for the Christmas meal not purchased. Our children were with us, though, and their Dad was home. We ordered in pizza for Christmas Eve dinner and had a wonderful time together.

When Christmas morning came, Murray had slept well and was still stable, so we praised the Lord and made breakfast. Our family Christmas mornings always included a hearty breakfast with everyone helping with the preparation and clean up. The stockings could usually be opened before breakfast, with the presents opened later, but we had no stockings this Christmas. That was okay. When we had lived in Minden, we'd attended a Christmas morning service at church before the presents, but there was no service this Christmas. So we opened the few gifts we found under the tree.

Christmas lunch consisted of a couple cans of tomato soup and bread. I found some food in the freezer to cook for our evening meal. It wasn't a traditional Christmas meal, but it was another great Christmas for our family.

FOUR
Hospital and Funeral

Murray returned to the London hospital on January 2, 1996 for more tests. Within three weeks, he was stable enough to come home. He stayed there until February 28, before returning to the Leamington hospital for another month.

He was gone by March 30.

As I travelled home from the hospital every evening in the month of March, my tears flowed as I talked with God. Many times I told Him what to do about the situation, asking for another miracle and the blessings that would follow. I don't think God minds His kids yelling at Him out their despair and grief.

After a few minutes of crying out, though, I would get it off my chest and settle down. Then I could talk to God in a more controlled manner, thanking Him for His involvement in the entire situation. I knew that none of this took Him by surprise.

Within fifteen minutes, I would be arriving home and asking His forgiveness for trying to tell Him just what to do. God always brought comfort and a good solid sleep.

Murray cheered aimlessly for his Toronto Maple Leafs. Nurses would move him to the next-door lounge to watch hockey games until the last week of March, when he watched the games on a TV in his private room. He was very ill, but he still cheered on his team, albeit to their frequent defeat.

Visitors marvelled at the encouragement Murray was during the month of March. Dave, one young man who visited, expressed how it went.

"I wanted to visit," Dave said. "I needed to visit, but I had never before visited anyone who was dying. I had no idea what to expect. I prayed my visit might bring him some encouragement; however, I came away more encouraged than I thought possible. A blessing indeed."

During the visit, Dave read a familiar passage of Scripture to Murray. After a couple of verses, he noticed that Murray was saying the verses along with him from memory. He was astounded that Murray then expounded on the passage.

Dave turned to another passage and the same thing happened.

We had several singsongs and prayer meetings in his room, as well as a few celebrations, snacks, and entire homemade meals. The goal was to keep him comfortable and make the most of these days.

Murray's dad made the trip to Leamington to say goodbye, as did Murray's siblings. The neighbours came, as well as church and community friends. And of course our children were there as often as possible. Five pastors in the area visited Murray that month, expressing their appreciation for his faithful support and work in the community.

His friend Bill sat every evening with him. They talked, laughed, read, prayed, or just sat quietly until Murray was ready to sleep.

Donna-Lee stayed with me that month and we took turns helping out to give each other breaks. My days at the hospital started at 8:00 a.m. Donna-Lee and I would leave around 8:00 p.m. when Bill arrived.

Friends brought gifts of food to our home. Many left messages of encouragement. We felt their prayers supporting us through each day. The regular happenings of daily life were on hold.

Three times that last month, we brought Murray home for a couple hours over the lunch hour. I would prepare a light meal that I knew he had enjoyed in the past. The last time, he asked to be taken back to the hospital early since he was in so much pain. He had only been moving the food around his plate, unable to eat.

Before leaving, though, he did check something under the hood of our car. That was on Wednesday. He passed on Saturday evening.

Nurses noticed Murray's bright demeanour, which shone through his pain and discomfort. I received a letter from one of the nurses following his death, expressing the staff's privilege in caring for him that month. She also mentioned that Murray's presence had attracted conversations between staff, whether or not they shared the same faith. The love of Jesus shining through Murray was compelling, encouraging believers and causing some to return to their faith in God. Others were challenged to examine their own lives considering God's love for them.

His funeral service was held in Minden. We also had a memorial service at our church in Leamington one week later. Many came. We appreciated everyone who took part and helped with arrangements and refreshments. His life was indeed celebrated.

A visit to the lawyer resulted in the paperwork moving along smoothly. My brother-in-law Everett, as a Hydro employee, looked after calls and many details. We very much appreciated the concern from Ontario Hydro with respect to helps available with the grieving process. I felt fortunate to be on the receiving end of so much help and concern.

At this time, I was advised by a few friends not to make any big life changes for at least a year. I listened and appreciated their concern.

However, God had other plans.

FIVE
Moving On

Soon after our marriage in 1966, Murray and I, knowing neither of us were super healthy, had a serious conversation about the possibility that one of us may pass before we had the opportunity to grow old together. We both gave the other permission to move ahead with life however we felt God lead, should that happen.

We filed this away in the recess of our minds and got on with life together, living it to the fullest.

When the dust settled from Murray's funeral, that thirty-year-old conversation resurfaced. I remember committing the rest of my life to God as I sat at a desk in my rearranged bedroom by the window. As a new widow, I asked Him to continue giving me direction and wisdom, praising Him for the comfort He was providing, knowing that Murray had lived a good, productive life and was now in the presence of our Lord. I felt okay with moving forward, whatever that involved.

The church board had been gracious regarding my absence from the office during March, and they were patient in waiting until I was ready to return.

I was back to work by mid-April. During that first week, I opened a letter from OMS International. We received letters from several organizations, but this one especially caught my eye since Murray and I had supported OMS for many years and knew several of their missionaries. The letter had been sent to supporters and advertised an open position with the organization: a Canadian prayer coordinator.

Don and Ivadel, the previous prayer coordinators, were known to me. I had received prayer and praise information from them for several years. I was also aware that this couple had stepped down during the past year to serve in a different capacity. At that time, I had thought about how great it would be to be able to serve in that area of ministry.

A staff member in the OMS Canada office had been filling in as much as she could, along with her own responsibilities, but now they were praying that God would move someone's heart to fill the position.

God had been preparing me for this for several decades and the time appeared to have finally come. I prayed about the possibility of this happening, knowing that it would bring several changes in my life.

Was this among the purposes behind the miracle God had provided on Worchester Avenue? Was I ready and prepared for the ongoing administration work that would be involved? Was I ready for the road and air travel, both in Canada and possibly beyond? Would I be able to represent the mission appropriately? Could I communicate effectively with supporters?

I pondered these questions for only a few days. God had already given me a sufficient portion of confidence when He provided the miracle. I knew I could respond in His strength.

I prayed. I applied.

While waiting for my acceptance, my car began to break down. A mechanic in our church assessed it and suggested that I should replace it.

This would be a new experience, I thought, having never bought a vehicle by myself before. I returned to the dealership where the car had been purchased. The same salesman, a person Murray had known and trusted, was available to help. I left with a gently used sporty two-door Buick Regal, complete with a colourful racing stripe along its side and only a few thousand miles on its odometer. It was white on the exterior and had an attractive baby blue interior. It also purred like a kitten. What a gem that little Buick was!

Years ago, Murray had given me a miniature replica of a big rig for my birthday. That little truck now rode with me in my back window. We were a sight for sore eyes. I still had an uncanny love for anything on wheels. Some vehicles, especially trucks of any size, still make my knees go weak.

I got the job at OMS Canada in May 1996, and in June I had the opportunity and privilege to attend the OMS International Conference held in Kentucky. One of my friends was happy to travel with me and attend the conference. Her husband had passed some time ago.

Off we went on a warm summer day the end of June.

Until this point, I had never pumped my own gas. There had always been someone else to do this job. Plus, most gas stations in Canada still offered this service in the 1990s and I availed myself of it. On our route in the United States, though, we were hard-pressed to find a station with gas-pumping staff.

Julie, my travel companion, was quite familiar with the gas pumps and did the honours on the first leg of our trip. By the time we returned five days later, I was more comfortable pumping gas as well. How thankful I was to Julie!

The conference was super encouraging and such a blessing to both of us. I renewed acquaintances, made new friends, and was commissioned during the closing conference service, along with several other new missionaries prepared for service in various places in the world. A board member from OMS United Kingdom offered the commissioning prayer for me.

OMS International has six sending countries, Canada being one of them. The Oriental Mission Society opened in the Orient in 1901. In war years, the organization sent missionaries to other countries as well and thus OMS spread to many parts of the world over the next decades. I felt honoured to be a part of this great organization.

Upon returning home, I set about the task of selling my home in Leamington. It was my desire to live closer to the Canadian OMS office in Hamilton.

This was another new experience, since I had never sold a home by myself. I sought the help of the same realtor from whom Murray and I had bought the home. He was aware of a woman who was looking for this very type and size of home. Within a couple of weeks, a sold sign hung outside my home on Worchester Avenue.

I offered my resignation at the church and planned to leave mid-August. The secretarial position had been such a good idea. Thank you, Murray! The position had reacquainted me with the experience of working outside the home.

The next project was to find somewhere else to live. Debra-Kaye accompanied me on the road trip to Burlington to find an apartment. We prayed for direction from God. A very suitable apartment was found on Lakeshore Boulevard along beautiful Lake Ontario. The apartment was rented with a move-in date for the end of August.

Even though our time in Leamington had only been a few years, Murray and I had made so many memories there, including great friendships, good and sad times, blessings and challenges, and lots of joy along the way.

There was much ahead of me, like sorting and packing, farewell lunches and parties, sending out change of address notices, etc. My children helped with moving items I no longer needed. Friends helped Andrew and Debra-Kaye pack the rental moving truck. Neighbours brought food and snacks.

My final activity on that last evening was a ride on the motorcycle of a good friend, Dan. What a great sendoff to Worchester Avenue!

I got help unloading in Burlington from friends with OMS and MFM. In no time, the truck was emptied and a welcoming meal provided. Andrew installed my new office furniture and set up my bed. Debra-Kaye helped with unpacking and placing throughout the home. They were soon on their way to return the moving truck. Breakfast food was in the kitchen, towels awaited me in the bathroom, and my bed was made. After another good night's sleep, I would be ready to start my life in Burlington and my new work.

Within a week, OMS Canada held its fall conference in the beautiful setting of Fair Havens near Beaverton. During lunch one day, Jeanine, an OMS missionary in Colombia, stood with me in the food line. She had heard of my story and told me how much it encouraged her. She went on share how God had completely healed her wounded and crippled hand as a young woman. In her ministry, she often put that hand on the shoulder of the person for whom she was going to pray. Her healed hand was a reminder to her of God's powerfulness. She would pray with assurance that God was hearing and would answer according to what He wanted to do in that person's life. Knowing how that miracle affected her life, she told me that she couldn't possibly imagine having a whole body healed.

It was my privilege to be Jeanine's driver the following week for a few days of ministry in eastern Ontario. What a blessing those days were! We laughed, prayed, got lost not once but twice, and enjoyed each other's company. I marvelled in her sharing of the awesome God-directed prison ministry in which she was involved in Colombia, and of her many opportunities to pray for those men as well as their families.

Jeanine went on to be a keynote speaker in secular and Christian prison conferences in many countries around the world.

The next few months were spent in the prayer department at the OMS mission office. I attended staff meetings, engaged in goal-setting, contacted our Canadian missionaries for prayer and praise info for the monthly prayer calendar, and forwarded urgent prayer requests to our supporters through snail mail, phone, and email.

So many long-time supporters of OMS assured me of their consistent prayers as I worked and travelled in the prayer ministry.

I have a vivid memory of a particular Sunday's afternoon missions prayer group in Elmira. I had gotten lost on my way there and was several minutes late. Afterward, our hosts assured me that they would especially pray for me in my travels. I made sure they always had my itinerary, so they knew when I was on the road. They were a special group.

That fall, I was introduced to the computer and embarked on a steep learning curve. I took several lessons from a young lady who was legally blind. She was a Bible college friend of Donna-Lee's and a great teacher. I appreciated her help. Before this, I barely knew how to turn on the machine.

On my schedule was an upcoming trip to the Maritimes to attend the fall board meetings and participate in a mission banquet. I also had speaking engagements for the mission in various parts of Ontario. In addition, I met the neighbours in my building, tried to keep up to speed with my adult children, visited Mom in Minden as often as possible, and took an active role in a new church. Life was exciting and rewarding. My health was great. My gratitude to God overflowed.

The Christmas season of 1996 came with its usual busyness. My apartment looked inviting with Christmas glitter. My little nativity scene, purchased so many years ago from Regal Gifts and Cards, took centre place. I enjoyed the artificial tree that Murray agreed to for his last Christmas.

All my children came to celebrate with me in Burlington. Donna-Lee had returned from her studies at Briercrest Bible College in western Canada. We visited my mom and other family members in Minden for a few days.

Murray had always enjoyed chocolate Turtles, even though some ingredients annoyed his compromised digestive system. As my children and I opened our box of Turtles that Christmas, it reminded us further of his absence. A family decision was made that we would always have Turtles at Christmas, in memory of their dad.

Often, as the years have gone by, everyone provides a box of Turtles. I'm always left with lots of Turtles to begin the new year.

SIX
The Lady in the Laundry Room

On a Saturday morning in late September 1996, I was gathering my laundry. As was my practice, I prayed for God's direction in any conversations waiting for me, adding a request that His name be glorified as I moved through the day. I proceeded to the laundry room of my apartment building.

When I entered the laundry room, there was only one lady there. She appeared to be of the same age and I could tell she was on the latter half of her laundry. We exchanged pleasantries about the weather, the laundry, and the fact that it was Saturday. It was a comfortable exchange.

I then decided to ask what occupied her time throughout the week. She informed me that she worked for a healthcare agency in the area. She also shared that her husband had passed about eighteen months previously. Following his death, she had sold the family home and moved into this apartment.

What a coincidence, I thought! I shot up a quick prayer for the ongoing conversation, then took my turn to inform her that my husband also had passed, and I too had sold my home and moved here in the past month.

I explained that I worked for a Christian mission as the prayer coordinator for Canada. Her response was that she needed to find another church. I had obviously given her the opportunity to open a topic close to her heart. At this point, I felt assured that God was indeed directing this conversation. I thanked Him and proceeded.

The woman told me that she had attended the church of her husband's family ever since they were married, but she didn't feel her spiritual needs were being met. She now visited her son out of town as often as she could on weekends. She enjoyed attending the church he and his young family attended. It was so different than her usual church, the one in which their children had been raised. The people really loved and cared for each other. The sermons were meaningful and made an impact on her heart and in people's daily lives. She wished there was a church like that in Burlington.

"Could you suggest one like that?" she asked.

I shared with her about my home church, asking whether she would like to attend with me. She indicated she had driven past that church many times but hadn't been able to muster enough nerve to leave her husband's family church to even visit another one.

While I would be happy to take her with me the next day, I would be away over the following few Sundays with work. But I suggested that she could meet some of the people and hear of the many available opportunities for fellowship.

When it was obvious she was getting ready to leave the laundry room, having folded her last few items, she said she was leaving town to visit her son for the rest of the weekend. She felt badly that she couldn't attend the next day.

Our pleasant time together ended rather abruptly, although I did tell her that I'd pray for her to enjoy her weekend away and that she would soon know what to do about her church life in Burlington.

We only exchanged first names. I didn't even ask where she lived in the rather large building.

As she left, I realized that I had no way of making further contact.

However, I knew God had opened the door, directed the conversation, and would continue the follow-up with whatever needed to be done in her life.

I didn't see her in the building after that. I did, however, often pray for her, asking God to help her find what she was looking for. I also prayed for some assurance of her spiritual salvation and that God would continue to direct her life.

I used my weekly trip down to the laundry room as a prayer trigger to pray for this woman.

That fall, I was away three Sundays every month. When I was able to be in my home church, I attended the missions elective class. I was often able to attend the midweek prayer meeting as well, which I thoroughly enjoyed.

This church was a very large one, busy with activities all week. For example, it offered fourteen adult elective classes Sunday mornings from which to choose and several Wednesday evening electives for adults. Many children and teen programs were available, too.

While attending meetings there, I couldn't help but think about how much the woman from the laundry room would also have enjoyed attending and how her needs could have been met at this church. I prayed as the Lord brought her face to my mind. I could do no more.

Soon 1997 arrived and during the winter months I didn't have as many Sunday meetings scheduled with the mission. In January, I decided to attend a Sunday adult class that offered a study that had particularly sparked my interest.

The class had already begun when I noticed a woman sitting directly across from me. She looked so familiar, but I couldn't place her. I must admit that I was distracted, trying to place this mystery lady, instead of giving my full attention to the teacher.

Just before the end of the class, it came to me: the woman from the laundry room was sitting directly across from me.

During the sharing time, she participated as if this was her class, speaking of prayer needs of people mentioned. She spoke like this was indeed her home church.

I anxiously waited for the class to finish and then approached her. She recognized me and we were pleased to meet again.

She had attended this church ever since a week following our discussion the previous September. She had enjoyed that first Sunday and met so many great people that it gave her the courage to make the move to a new home church. In the fall of 1996, she found what she was looking for. Her elective classes both on Sundays as well as midweek were different than the ones I had attended, and it's very easy to miss someone in such a large church.

We often underestimate the value of giving our day to God and asking His daily direction. Would I have missed the opportunity of sharing in her life had I not listened to God's prompting that fall day in 1996? What about the lives she has touched since then, with her concern and enthusiasm to help others in their spiritual walk? I am so pleased that our lives are God's business and we are only asked to be faithful.

The apostle Paul, in Colossians 3, speaks of the new life in Christ as well as guidelines for Christian households. He then offers further instructions:

> Devote yourselves to prayer, being watchful and thankful. And pray for us, too, that God may open a door for our message, so that we may proclaim the mystery of Christ, for which I am in chains. Pray that I may proclaim it clearly, as I should. Be wise in the way you act toward outsiders; make the most of every opportunity. Let your conversation be always full of grace, seasoned with salt, so that you may know how to answer everyone. (Colossians 4:2–6)

The story of this woman reminds me of the importance of committing each day and activity to God and asking His direction for even minute details in our everyday living, so that He will open the door of opportunity, in His way and in His time. He is the king of creativity!

God is never too busy to lead us to a person who needs a listening ear, positive suggestion, gentle push, fervent prayer, warm smile, cup of tea, tender hug, and shoulder on which to lean while sharing a tear together. What a privilege we have, as believers in the Lord Jesus Christ, to pray for others and be involved in their lives! God is the engineer of our lives, even on laundry day.

SEVEN
Prayer Ministry Activity

The responsibilities of a missions prayer coordinator involve recruiting prayer support and informing constituents of ongoing prayer needs and praise notes. It's also important to provide updates to answered prayer requests, as much as possible. We had dear prayer warriors across Canada who faithfully prayed. How precious they were! What an enjoyment it was to meet them, sit and discuss their faith journeys, share a meal, and ask God's continued blessing on their lives.

I discovered some seasoned Christians in our country, in churches of all denominations, who hadn't yet availed themselves of the wonderful world of prayer. Part of my ministry was to share this opportunity to encourage them to delve into prayer. It was always encouraging to revisit these churches, groups, and individuals later and hear from those who had gone deeper with their prayer life.

While planning for air travel with the prayer ministry, my practice was to pray to be seated where God would have me sit. Sometimes my seat was changed by a flight attendant at the last moment, or I was moved from economy to business class for one reason or another.

On one flight from Saskatchewan, I prayed to be able to shut my eyes and rest. The day before, a cold took hold of my body and I didn't feel capable of conversing intelligently with anyone. My desire was granted with a row of seats to myself.

For all my other flights, I had conversations with interesting people.

A grandmother, returning from a visit with her grandchildren, was desperate to share her burden with someone who would listen, understand, and pray.

A mine worker reminded me of my son Dwight. This worker was returning from a major project and was pleased to have a motherly woman with whom to talk and unwind, albeit a stranger.

An elderly man was a believer and delighted in having another Christian to pass the time in conversation.

A young lady was interested in my work and ultimately interested in faith in God.

A teenage girl needed to hear an alternative to her questionable lifestyle.

A businessman spent a huge chunk of his time on planes, usually working on his projects while flying. However, on a certain flight home he was happy to have someone with whom to talk about everyday life.

A young mother with two young children in tow appreciated having someone to entertain one of them for a while.

Often the waits at airports, or flight delays, also provided unexpected opportunities for meaningful conversations.

I represented OMS at community mission banquets, constituent breakfasts, retreats and conferences, as well as monthly prayer groups. This work energized my soul. I worked from my home office as well as the Canadian office in Hamilton. I enjoyed these challenges! Preparing for every meeting took blocks of time, but I was often surprised by what God brought to my mind while speaking, and often sharing my testimony. I would remember certain aspects of what He was doing through our missionaries around the world, or bringing to mind parts of my own life I hadn't thought of for years.

On one occasion, a woman said to me, "I'm looking forward to what you share when you speak today."

"Thank you," I replied. "I am too."

Every time I diverted from what I had prepared, at least one person in the audience would comment afterward on that very part of the presentation, telling me it was what she or he had needed to hear that day.

I had an opportunity to share my testimony on *100 Huntley Street* in the late fall of 1996, in a segment to be aired on Boxing Day. A family in Minden was searching for something to watch on Boxing Day and happened to land on the program just as the facilitator announced that Phyllis Sisson would be up next. Their normal viewing didn't include a broadcast such as this, but they watched it with interest since they knew of our family.

One never knows how, who, or what might touch a person's life. I continued to give God the glory for what He was doing.

In January 1997, I met Gord. He would become my second husband in September of that same year. We were both attending the same elective class at church and met at the coffee table. He was a human resource specialist and was gearing up for early retirement from his hospital job.

Gord's wife had passed in 1996, and following retirement he joined OMS Canada as assistant to the Canadian executive director. Within a year, he was appointed the director position. The work kept him in the Canadian office a good percentage of the time, whereas my work was divided evenly in three ways: in our home office, the mission office, and on the road.

Gord travelled as often as required to various Christian schools across Canada, for conferences and special events for OMS and to meet with those interested in serving. He also spoke in churches to present opportunities for service either on the home front or in foreign countries. He also acted in a pastoral role to missionaries on home assignment as they settled in Ontario for their homebase.

He performed well in this capacity and enjoyed working beyond his first retirement. We often worked elbow to elbow in the home office, staying up to date on correspondence, preparing documents and reports, and drafting information for quarterly or annual mailouts. At our office, we often burned the midnight oil.

I had a document on the wall of our home entitled "Office Hours." It summed up what it was like in the office, especially working in a ministry context with people around the world.

Open most days about 9 or 10, occasionally as early as 7, but some days as late as 12 or 1. We close about 5:30 or 6, occasionally about 4 or 5, but sometimes as late as 11 or 12. Some days we aren't here at all, but lately we've been here just about all the time, except when we are someplace else.

I thoroughly enjoyed that decade of work, both in offices and travelling, whether in Canada or abroad. God was fulfilling my desires. It was so enjoyable that it didn't seem like work. The bonus was seeing God at work in people's lives.

On one of my trips to the Maritimes, I was asked to visit a young woman in hospital with muscular dystrophy. She was twenty-five years old and had accepted Jesus into her life as a young teen. The prognosis was not in her favour and she had spent a lot of time in hospital in recent years, interrupting her high school studies.

"I've finally graduated from Grade Twelve," she told me when I visited her.

She was such an inspiration to all who visited, as well as the hospital staff. I left the hospital more encouraged than I could have imagined.

She passed a couple weeks later. I was privileged to have met her.

There were many highlights from my decade with the prayer ministry. An interesting one was sharing with the Theologically Hip college and career group in Calgary, Alberta. That afternoon, I went hiking with Grace, who attended the group and had applied to work in the OMS office. We had an invigorating hike and much fellowship together.

Later that evening, I joined the group for a carry-in supper. They asked great questions and were interested in my miracle from a theological perspective.

Another time, a knitting club in Saint John, New Brunswick invited me to join them even though I didn't knit. They wished to hear my story. So I spoke while they knitted. They were rather a secluded group and had been meeting together for twenty-some years. Apparently, I was their first non-knitter. I felt privileged.

I had an interesting opportunity to speak to a rotary club in Ontario one November. The month of November is the annual awareness month to eradicate polio worldwide. When I started talking, there was quiet chattering in the audience. Before long, as I continued speaking, there was absolute silence. They were intrigued with what they heard. I'm not sure what they were used to hearing from guest speakers!

After sharing my story, I weaved in details of the miracle of salvation. I also challenged their chapter to consider supporting polio survivors in need of assistance with equipment to help them cope with the late effects of polio.

I seldom received such a positive review as I did from that group.

It was rewarding to visit and encourage parents of single daughters serving abroad. It gave my motherly heart a boost.

I was once blessed to provide hospitality and a tour of Niagara Falls for a young Hungarian girl who had served as our translator while in Vac and Budapest.

I was also encouraged while visiting retired OMS missionaries across Canada. I got to share at a home meeting in Montreal Lake, Saskatchewan where several families filled a living room. Children quietly filtered in and out, having their own time in the lower recreation room. The evening ended with a scrumptious carry-in meal, enjoyed by all.

We took a group picture and the sea of faces still brings a smile to my face with the reminder of God's goodness.

One of my long-term goals to entering this ministry was to increase the number of people interesting in, and praying for, OMS missionaries around the world. Within a few years, the number of people praying had tripled. Personally making contact and spending time with people was most effective. Our recruitment had also increased. I give God the glory for what He was doing in the ministry.

As time has passed, much of the personal contact with supporters has diminished for various reasons. This saddens me.

PJ and Darlene in Ecuador in 1996.

Gord and Phyllis in 1997.

Phyllis in the Rocky Mountains, British Columbia in 1997.

PJ and Mom at Niagara Falls, Ontario in 1997.

*Mom's eightieth birthday celebration with
Joy, Steve, Mom, Darlene, PJ, Gord, Bernice, and Keith in 2000.*

EIGHT
Travel Abroad

For nine years, from the late fall of 1997 through the fall of 2006, Gord and I travelled together for several weeks. While in Great Britain, we visited many churches, prayer groups, and Men for Missions gatherings. We participated in three retreats. What great times of fellowship, encouragement, and spiritual growth we had!

We also met many long-time supporters of OMS. We had tea with a special lady with the OMS UK board. In 1996, she had offered the commissioning prayer for me at the OMS international conference in the United States.

We were invited to people's homes and fed like royalty. The hospitality was superb. I enjoyed seeing where our friends in this part of the world lived and enjoyed worshipping in their churches.

I also noticed several big rigs on the roads. A bright pink truck and hauler was the most attractive piece of machinery I had ever seen.

Bill and Kathleen, who were the OMS UK executive directors at the time, provided lodging, many meals, and transportation for us throughout England, Northern Ireland, Scotland, and Wales. They were such gracious hosts and we enjoyed our time with them immensely.

In total, Gord and I spent twenty-one days in Great Britain. Gord brought greetings from Canada and spoke at several Sunday morning services, as well as with a Men for Missions gathering. I spoke twenty-five times to a variety of prayer groups. I had the opportunity to share my testimony for a three-part radio program to be aired over the following three weeks.

We then enjoyed a couple of days of sightseeing. Our tour included a visit to the large Harrods store as well as seeing the sights around the beautiful city of London. We were able to also watch the changing of the guard ceremony at Buckingham Palace.

On our last day, we flew to Paris for a six-hour visit. We sat under the Eiffel Tower, saw many delightful sights, and had a lovely lunch on an outdoor patio. Our travel agent in Ontario had been instrumental in arranging for a taxi driver in Paris. This Chinese Christian was fluent in English and happy to offer his services for a minimal fee. He asked us many questions about Canada and we had sweet fellowship with him. He was very informative about Paris. The afternoon visit was so much fun and further fulfilled my innermost desire to meet people and see other parts of the world.

We visited and shared in many other countries where our missionaries served, including Hungary, Spain, Mozambique, South Africa, Mexico, and Ecuador. God was working in so many creative ways. There were missionaries to meet, Christians with whom to spend time, new foods to sample, modes of travel to experience, and awesome landscapes of every description to see with our own eyes. We visited churches, schools, camps, hospitals, homes, and markets in busy cities and remote villages, both in areas where the well-off thrived and those where people barely survived. We had the opportunity to show our appreciation to our OMS missionaries for their faithful service, brought greetings from OMS Canada office staff and board of directors, and represent faithful supporters across Canada.

By visiting these countries, we could better answer the questions of Canadians who were interested in part-time or full-time service with OMS. The trips also bolstered my enthusiasm to share with interested Canadians up-to-date prayer needs, answers to prayer, and reports from the missionaries they supported.

Another privilege was a five-week teaching trip to Kazakhstan under the umbrella of Intervarsity Christian Fellowship. We also visited the small country of Liechtenstein, crossed the southern part of Germany, and travelled in Austria. What beautiful countries and people!

Gord had always desired to visit the Matterhorn, a mountain in the Alps along the Italian-Swiss border. The large pyramidal peak has a summit of 14,692 feet, one of the highest in Europe.

The day we were there was beautiful, clear, very cold, and sunny. We were able to drive as far as vehicles were allowed, then took the shuttle to the village and proceeded to the ski lift. Many seasoned skiers were going up, along with a few tourists like Gord and me. We ascended as high as possible on the ski lift, then walked around and enjoyed the glistening snow and terrain. The skiers were a sight as they prepared to ski down the mountain.

We enjoyed a hot drink in the chalet and admired the breathtaking view of this striking mountain—that is, until the last call for the trip down by ski lift. We then enjoyed our trip back to the ground below... but not before I lost my prescription sunglasses. They will be forever buried in the snows of the Matterhorn.

We travelled to Africa with our good friends Mark and Ruth. On this trip, we were able to visit a missionary friend named Danny in Zimbabwe. Danny had been a close friend of Gord's and Mark's since childhood. Gord often talked of the three of them as youngsters and the antics they'd gotten into, including terrorizing their Sunday school teachers. It was so good to see the three of them enjoy each other's company in Zimbabwe.

Danny and his wife had set out to be career missionaries in Africa. At the time of our visit, he had been in Zimbabwe for thirty-seven years, establishing churches and orphanages. He and his wife had four sons, all of them born there.

Sadly, his wife had died in a car accident when the youngest son was still a preschooler. Danny had persevered.

Their sons were in Zimbabwe, too, with a couple of them in ministry, following in their dad's footsteps.

I was asked to share my testimony in two churches, a home study group, and a ladies prayer group. Gord took part in a church service where one of Danny's sons was the pastor.

In Mozambique, we had an awesome experience at a church service held in an African hut. The congregation of about eighty-five people boasted all ages from the very young to the very elderly. As they crowded in, I watched a sweet little girl under the age of one crawl around the sea of feet. Young children sat on their parent' laps or squished between them on benches. Teens, standing or sitting, listened intently.

The worship leader that morning was a Bible college student who had been born without the use of his legs. He couldn't stand or experience the enjoyment of walking, instead moving around with the use of his hands. He hopped up on a chair at the front of the church that morning and joyfully led us in beautiful worship. He had a wonderful singing voice.

I had been asked to share my testimony. The twelve-year-old daughter of one of the missionaries translated for me. She did a terrific job, given the fact she had only recently learned to speak the language.

Following the service, the worship leader expressed his appreciation in hearing my testimony. He praised God for the miracle, then pulled on his rubber gloves and crawled along a muddy pathway. Some would say that if anyone ever needed a miracle, it would be that young man. But he was just encouraged to hear of God's miracle in my life.

I heard a few years later that he had graduated from Bible college and was pastoring a church in that same area. He owned a wheelchair now. What a testimony that young man has!

Everywhere I went, my story preceded me. It was a joy to share God's faithfulness before and following the miracle on Worchester Avenue. God was indeed fulfilling my desire to visit more countries on my big world map through a ministry of encouragement. He went above and beyond the highest expectations I could ever have imagined for myself.

My sister-in-law Darlene accompanied me to Australia and New Zealand. We participated in several events there, including a ladies community craft event, representing Canada at the ninetieth-year celebration of OMS New Zealand, offering the prayer at a church's annual mission banquet, sharing with a group of people ready to embark on a Men for Missions trip overseas, enjoying a meal with the New Zealand staff, and attending a special Mother's Day service.

Darlene and I took a one-day bus excursion in Australia. We also toured the northern island of New Zealand. We enjoyed seeing the beauty of both of these countries.

At five years old, I had first seen Australia on the lower right-hand side of my big world map. Fifty-five years later, I was there.

Darlene and I were both sixty the year of that trip. It was our special birthday celebration together. She passed in the fall of 2021 after a year of struggling with complications following a serious back surgery. I miss her!

PJ in Kazakhstan in 1998.

PJ in the Swiss Alps in 1998.

PJ in South Africa in 1999.

PJ in Scotland in 2002.

PJ in the mountains of Ecuador in 2003.

PJ on the Great Ocean Road in Australia in 2005.

NINE
Kazakhstan

Prior to any trip, whether in Canada or overseas, my practice was to enlist the prayer support of at least one hundred people. Stan, a dear missionary friend, once said, "Sometimes the hand of God is moved by the prayer of one person. Other times it takes a nation." I always erred on the side of much prayer support to carry me through my time and ministry with OMS. I knew the enemy of the gospel wasn't happy with anyone participating in God's work around the world and would throw his nasty darts one way or another to try to thwart their eternal progress. He shudders at a head bowed in prayer and a heart reaching out to God. Prayer is the best defence a believer has.

In October 1998, I enlisted my prayer partners as Gord and I jetted off to Kazakhstan. It was a long flight and we were advised to take a layover in Austria for a few days to catch up on jetlag, since we would be busy immediately upon reaching Kazakhstan.

In Austria, we checked into our well-guarded hotel and had fifteen hours of solid sleep. We then had a couple days to see some of the beautiful sights of Vienna and taste the delicious food of this country. We were even able to see a live Austrian opera. How delightful!

When we flew into the city of Almaty in southeast Kazakhstan, we had part of a day and one night—once again, in a well-guarded hotel. What a beautiful city! We also got to do some sightseeing with the vice-president of the university where we would be involved for the next five weeks.

It was quite an experience to fly northeast to the large city of Ust-Kamenogorsk. The plane no doubt would have been grounded in North America, but after loading our own luggage and praying for safety we took off, arriving without incident at our destination.

Kazakhstan is the largest breakaway country from the former Soviet Union and has a strong Muslim population. Kazakh University in Ust-Kamenogorsk had about thirteen thousand students that year across several campuses. We visited the Kazakh American Business College campus, which had approximately one hundred students. They were required to have a certain level of understanding of English to enter and expected to be fluent upon graduation. Most were able to converse in English to some degree as first-year students, while a few were quite fluent already. The goal of most students attending this college was to excel in the business world, allowing them to travel and work wherever they chose afterward. Knowing English was a must.

Canada was among the countries from which the school drew teachers. That fall, Gord was enlisted to teach a fourth-year course in human resources. I taught a conversational English class with first-year students.

When we arrived on October 28, the weather was beautiful with crisp coloured leaves on the ground. We felt right at home.

About a week later, the temperatures dropped quickly and snow covered the ground.

By the second week of November, the thermometer often read -30°F

Within another week, it read -40°F. Snappy and crunchy! We left our coats on in class, along with wearing warm boots and sometimes those typical Russian furry hats. The heat in the dorm where we were housed was enough to keep the water pipes from freezing—usually. Cold showers often greeted us on frigid mornings. The coldest morning was -45°F.

The little fridge didn't keep milk or cream sweet overnight, so I learned how to drink my coffee black and looked forward to that hot cup every morning.

A student who had some culinary courses under her belt was assigned to cook our evening meals. This really added to our appreciation of the country.

We found an American pizza restaurant in the city called Pizza Blues, which always played music by Louis Armstrong in the background.

Friday evenings became our special date night at Pizza Blues. We made friends with a few of the waiters and waitresses and had conversations with them in broken English.

Many of our acquaintances there asked why anyone would leave Canada to come to Kazakhstan, especially in the winter. We took the opportunity to share what had motivated us.

About the middle of November, I felt desperate for a haircut. Looking around the mall for a hair salon didn't prove helpful, and we didn't have access to a good pair of scissors.

One evening, I asked Gord to trim my hair with the only tool available: toenail clippers. What fun we had! And the haircut didn't look too bad at all. I think he missed his calling.

When we returned home and visited my hairdresser, he didn't know whether to laugh or cry at hearing the story.

My mandate while teaching the conversational English course was simply to throw out a subject and have the students discuss it. We were advised not to share our faith in the classroom. And yet the first question asked, after everyone was introduced, came from a young man whom I'll call Lee: "Do you believe in God?"

I breathed a quick prayer and answered. Thus started five weeks of discussion, in English, mostly between this young man and me. I soon discovered that he had some kind of control over the class. The others spoke only when they received his nod.

Lee's only sibling had been murdered two weeks prior to our arrival. His brother, a fourth-year student, had been the first young man to become a believer in Jesus on this campus through the ministry of Intervarsity. That had happened about three months earlier.

Their parents were divorced and the two brothers had been very close, but now Lee was alone. He was angry at this God of whom his brother spoke. My motherly heart went out to him. I just wanted to hold him close and comfort him, but of course that wouldn't have been appropriate.

So we conversed in English. He had many great questions to which he insisted on hearing answers. He made comments driven by his anger, needing to vent. I did a lot of listening. Sometimes he allowed others to comment, and often they broke into their own language for a while. I would bring them back to the purpose of the class and keep them practicing their English in dialogue.

A lot of our discussion during those five weeks revolved around Christianity, at their request. Meanwhile, I constantly sensed the prayers of my supporters in Canada.

During our stay in Ust-Kamenogorsk, I had an opportunity to share my story in a Korean missionary church. This was a multicultural congregation, with every sentence I spoke being translated into Korean, Kazakh, and Russian by three translators. I had become quite adept at speaking with a single translation. Waiting for each of my comments to be translated in three languages, however, tested my patience and stretched the limits of my memory.

We developed a good relationship with the young teacher who had invited us to this church. She accompanied me one day to buy a warmer coat and escorted us around the city on the weekends. She also wanted us to share a meal with her and her mother.

We travelled by bus to their home on a very frosty day. They lived on the third floor of an apartment building and the stairwells leading to their lovely apartment was cold, dark, and narrow. Their windows were frozen about three-quarters of the way up and this was November. We were told that the windows wouldn't thaw until spring.

The temperature inside the apartment was quite cold, but the fellowship was warm. A sweet little boy of about four wandered into the apartment when the meal was ready to be served. He lived in one of the other apartments, and apparently came over some days when he was hungry. He was welcomed and another plate was set. They served a delicious Russian meal! We felt honoured.

When this part of the former Soviet Union broke off to form Kazakhstan, its people were encouraged to learn Kazakh. However, our friend's mother never had, believing she was too old to master a new language. Instead she was living for the day when one of her children could move her across the border to Russia.

I heard a few years later that she and her daughter did make that move. They settled in Moscow, where her daughter found a teaching position. The teacher was fluent in English, Russian, and Kazakh and was indeed a delightful young lady.

We were invited for a house church service in Ust-Kamenogorsk, where a large group of believers met regularly. Chairs were placed in rows in every room on the main floor, each one facing the living room. The main floor had several small rooms partitioned with walls and narrow doorways. However, placing the chairs so they faced the living room helped the attendees feel like they were all together, participating and listening to what was being said "at the front." There was no sound system or musical instruments and the house was full of people of all ages. They felt privileged to have a church to attend. These people were quiet and listened intently to every word spoken. They sang every note of every hymn.

I had been asked to share my testimony. The fellow who had invited us to teach at the college served as my translator. As I shared the part of my story where God had placed the people of Russia on my heart, I noticed tears running down the cheeks of a woman with a beige furry Russian hat. I spoke of having heard of the many hardships families in Russia faced and I often prayed for them as God prompted me.

Following the service, I spoke to this woman through our translator. Her family was one of many whose father had been taken away, never to be seen again. This Christian family, however, had sensed the prayers of God's people elsewhere in the world. Her mother had kept the family together even though she was unable to work. Somehow food had come their way and they had survived.

It now blessed her heart to hear that someone in Canada had been praying during those difficult years! I was only one person, but to her I represented many who must have been praying. Meeting this woman was worth all the cold nights, sour milk, challenging flights, hours of jetlag, and rough experiences during the fall of 1998.

The evening before we left Ust-Kamenogorsk, I was informed that Lee had received Jesus into his life. I learned a couple of years later that he was growing in his faith and his father had also accepted Christianity.

Much ministry happened in Kazakhstan as Canadians partnered in prayer.

When we left Ust-Kamenogorsk and were clearing customs in Almaty, I noticed a cut on my thumb. I had no idea how it had happened. My high tolerance level to pain hadn't served me well, since I couldn't remember when I got the wound.

An official in uniform told me that I would have to come with him. He didn't give me time to question why we were going or where, but his demeanour was demanding. He took me through a crowded corridor and ushered me into a dimly lit room with one chair and a little wobbly table. He told me to stay there until the doctor came.

Can you imagine what all went through my mind as I waited those ten very long minutes? I prayed for protection! Before coming here, I had been searching for a tissue to wrap around my thumb to stop the blood from getting on everything I touched. In so doing, I had handed my pouch with my ticket and identification and passport to Gord. It had remained in his possession as I was quickly ushered away.

The doctor arrived wearing a white coat. He spoke in broken English and asked what had happened to my thumb. He wasn't impressed with my answer.

He assessed my condition and took some products from his little black bag. Then he cleansed the wound with a little bottle in his bag and wrapped my thumb in bandage, just like my favourite teacher would have done in that little red schoolhouse where I'd spent my first year at school. The doctor then told me to sit in that room until someone came to escort me back to the gates.

Sure enough, after another long ten-minute wait, an official-looking person came to return me. In retrospect, I was grateful for the interest shown for my wellbeing, although the experience was rather unsettling.

TEN
Adventures

During my time with OMS, I often visited countries where guards, often with various kinds of guns, stood by store doors, in hotels, and inside banks. This initially took a little getting used to.

Armed officials would operate road checks. In Ecuador, I was chosen to be taken to the guardhouse for no reason I could determine. Darlene and I had been driving with a local when this official stopped us. We sat on the side of the road for fifteen minutes, watching the faces of the men in the guardhouse. We heard outbursts of laughter as they looked my direction. That was unsettling.

My passport was finally returned by another man in uniform who wore an annoying grin on his face. We thankfully got back on our way.

While walking through a crowded area in a beautiful city in Spain, a female police officer touched my elbow and said, in perfect English, "Excuse me, ma'am, but I saw a man riffling through your purse. He just ran off. Can you please check to see if anything is missing?"

I immediately felt thankful for some words of wisdom I'd heard from a missionary friend regarding how and where to place documents and money in my purse so a thief would have the least opportunity to quickly find them.

Nothing was missing.

This officer had been walking behind me with several people between us when she saw the potential thief. She knew what to look for in such a crowd; I was thankful for her concern, and also thankful for my prayer supporters.

In Ecuador, while taking pictures of an area of the town where Darlene lived, an armed uniformed man tapped me on the shoulder. As I turned to him, he pointed to my camera and said something in Spanish. I didn't understand what he was saying and told him so, but he kept speaking very sternly.

Anxiety rose in my chest as he kept pointing at my camera.

Just then, Darlene came back from her errand in a nearby store. She knew him personally and greeted him, introducing me as Morley's sister. They began a lengthy conversation, and at one point Darlene said "No, no, no" with a smile on her face.

When they finished, she took me by the arm and told me that we had to leave. She explained to me that the man had thought I was taking pictures of the army base and feared the pictures would fall into the wrong hands. He had intended to destroy my camera and escort me to jail. That's when she had said "No, no, no" and proceeded to say that it certainly wouldn't be necessary. She had needed to convince him that I was just an interested visitor, snapping pictures, adding that I was very much enjoying their town and meeting their people, and reminding him that he had known her husband, Morley.

She promised I wouldn't take any more pictures. I was encouraged to never return to this town again.

On another visit to Ecuador, an election was taking place. We were confined to our hotel the day of the vote for our own protection.

We travelled the next day to a nearby area, where a missionary friend and I dropped into a coffee shop for tea. We were enjoying our visit when we heard a very loud noise on the street. The owner of the restaurant quickly shut the heavy shutters and locked the doors.

No one inside seemed too excited.

"We'll be okay," my friend said. "There's a group of rioters coming down the street. They will be supporters of the party who didn't win the election. It's quite normal for riots to break out in the country everywhere following an election. They'll break windows without shutters and steal whatever they wish to in their anger. The heavy shutters will keep us safe. We'll just stay here awhile until it's safe to go into the streets again."

She had experienced such things and worse over her many years serving in that country. She was as calm as a cucumber.

While in Mexico City, I ventured downtown with a large group of people. This enormous district covers an area of almost four square miles. There were several national festivals going on, as apparently there often were. I was keenly aware of a perceived evil presence all around us with the people's endless chanting. I claimed the protection of our Lord.

I can't say that I ever mellowed to these negative and sometimes frightful experiences, but I learned to rest in the comfort of knowing that God had orchestrated these trips for His reasons. We were always travelling to support the missionaries. The safest place a Christian can be is at the centre of His will.

In Mozambique, I had the opportunity to speak with a group of six women one Saturday afternoon. These were hard-working women, trying to keep food on the tables for their families. Once a month, they met in someone's home to have a Bible study on their only free afternoon and pray. These women knew how to pray. Oh, how they prayed! They were such loving and interesting women. They served a light lunch and I came away blessed beyond words.

In South Africa, a Christian man drove Gord and I where we were to go. We had three days before going on to Mozambique. Our driver was originally from Wales and had married a woman from South Africa. She was a teacher in the Catholic school attached to the church.

We attended Mass and enjoyed the inspirational worship service. We were then asked to speak to the Grades Seven and Eight classes about Canada.

I took Grade Seven. What a great group of young people! They were very mature. Their questions were about Canada and much Intelligent discussion followed. When I shared briefly about the miracle in my life, the students asked about why God would heal me without me even asking for it, when others who do ask to be healed are not. Good question! This deep topic would require more time. I prayed their teachers would use this opportunity to discuss the matter further.

Later that afternoon, we visited a hospital for precious AIDS babies, all under the age of six. We held them. They had been dropped off at the hospital as infants because no one wanted them. The nurses were extremely special to care for and love these children until their short lives were over. They appreciated the time we spent with the babies and toddlers, and they also appreciate our prayers for their ministry. The day wrapped up with a feast of pancakes with a delicious array of toppings in a nearby church. It was Pancake Tuesday.

While in Zimbabwe, Gord and I visited an orphanage outside the city where young children were housed in thatched-roof structures. Each home had at least one adult living with them. Danny, the missionary who took us there, had brought a large bag of freshly picked corn as well as candies. The children were very gracious and courteous while receiving the candy. They would each enjoy a half-cob of freshly cooked corn along with their evening meal. This was special for them! Corn was more often cooked into a gruel, similar in appearance to mashed potatoes, and was very nourishing for these little people.

When we left, as many as possible ran behind our vehicle as far as they could, yelling, smiling, and waving. You can imagine that my motherly heart wanted to hug each one of those precious children.

I thanked God for the opportunity to visit so many countries and to meet these interesting and loving people, to see their homes and share their meals and speak in their churches. I was blessed to share with their families and bring a ministry of encouragement.

God continued to do more than I could ever imagine in my life as an able-bodied woman, and He only asked me to be faithful.

ELEVEN
Grandchildren

Grandchildren are a blessing from the Lord. Some say that if they had known grandchildren were so great, they would have had them first! I believe they are fascinating little people who reflect the characteristics of such a variety of family members, yet they have their own unique personalities. How creative God was when He initiated families!

Within a period of four years, four granddaughters were born in our family. Kyla was Dwight and Donna's firstborn, arriving while Gord and I were on our honeymoon in 1997. Gord liked to tell the story that he took his bride on the honeymoon and returned with a grandmother.

Caitlin and Alyssa were born in 1999, three months apart, to Debra-Kaye and Andrew and Dwight and Donna respectively. That was an exciting and busy year for everyone, including Grandma.

Madison, sister to Caitlin, was the last of that quartet of granddaughters, born at the end of December 2001.

I had the privilege of being at the hospital for each of their births. I heard their first cries and held each of the precious little bundles with their various looks and personalities already shining through their bright eyes. These are indeed highlights of my life.

Dean and Jennifer's three children were born between 2007 and 2011. They are Luke, Hannah, and James. James is the only baby I didn't see as soon as he was born. At the time, I had a commitment I couldn't change, but I made the three-hour trip north as soon as possible. I remember receiving a speeding ticket en route! The officer was understanding of my urgency, but he still wrote the ticket. He suggested that I slow down so I could arrive safely to meet my new grandson. I did.

These three children were all born unique, missing material from the thirteenth chromosome. Each is precious and has been blessed with a loving and compassionate spirit, which often shines through.

All my grandchildren are in my thoughts and prayers daily—for protection, blessing, wisdom, and direction from our heavenly Father. I entrust each one to God.

The prayers of my own grandmother when I was four years old, and beyond, often remind me of my privilege—and yes, my responsibility—to support my children in prayer with the raising of their own children. As my grandchildren grow into adulthood, my prayers never cease.

My years with OMS took me away from my family often. This could have been a challenge. Had I not been assured that God was directing me to be involved with the ministry of encouragement, I would not have been able to go with a clear conscience. In return, God has allowed me many special experiences with my grandchildren, individually and together at family gatherings. Laughter often rules the day.

TWELVE
The Years After OMS

Gord and I decided that we would both step down from OMS when he was about to celebrate his sixty-fifth birthday. We retired in 2006 when the OMS board of directors met for their fall meetings. We had both thoroughly enjoyed our time serving with the mission, felt a sweet fulfillment of service to our Lord, met so many great people in various countries, and witnessed God at work in people's lives. We were ready to move on into the next phase of our lives, whatever that would hold.

I opened a cleaning service in Strathroy. Cleaning was another of my passions and I knew this would be a good venture. I wasn't ready to just retire; that could come a few years down the road.

I bathed the notion in prayer, and I was sixty-two when my cleaning business opened. I was still in good health and I anticipated having just a few homes to clean and ample time to serve in our home church. I never expected the business to grow as it did.

My first client owned a five-thousand-square-foot home along with a large indoor pool. As she viewed my resume, she asked about my previous work. When I explained about my involvement with OMS, she seemed surprised.

"I'm afraid you will find cleaning homes rather boring," she said.

I assured her that I had appreciated that decade of my life, but now I looked forward to fulfilling another of my passions.

As my business got off the ground, I searched for an effective chemical-free product to use. Within six months, I had found one. Karen, a friend who was also a client, introduced me to Norwex, a company out of Norway that was fast becoming a contender in Canada.

As I started to clean with these products, more doors opened by word of mouth. Some clients sought to remove chemical-laden cleaning products as much as possible for a variety of reasons. Only one client wasn't totally pleased with the products. She admitted that her home was sparkling clean, but she missed the chemical smell!

I hired part-time staff before the end of the first year since I had more homes and clients than I could handle alone. Debra-Kaye worked well with me, and by the third year we were cleaning for forty-nine families—some weekly, others biweekly, as well as four businesses on a regular basis.

In total, my staff included seven women and two men.

I was in my glory. I loved the challenge of meeting new clients, cleaning, and assuring that all work was done well. I also enjoyed scheduling staff. God was using this business in ways I would have thought unimaginable. On the side of my SUV, my contact information was printed alongside a quote from Psalm 100. Several interested people inquired as to what that was about, providing an opportunity for me to share with them.

While my cleaning service was getting underway, Gord's health went downhill. This began with mini-strokes and a quadruple bypass surgery. His recovery did not go well. Not only did his overall well-being suffer, but I watched as his behaviour and personality slowly changed. I enlisted a few personal prayer supporters and was so very thankful for their prayers, understanding, and practical help during this time.

At our church, I looked after a Sunday school department for children between the ages of four and five. We had four teams of teachers and helpers, with a minimum of twenty-five children present each Sunday, and often more than thirty. We eventually ran the program during both morning worship services.

The children were livewires and such a delight to be with. I loved them all. Debra-Kaye served in the nursery department of the same church. It was special to work together with her in the children's ministry. I served in this area for a few years—that is, until Gord became restless and unsettled, wanting to seek out other churches.

Gord's actions varied from day to day. I knew this wasn't normal behaviour for him, and I also knew he couldn't help it. We went to appointments with a variety of doctors, and I sought help from an agency who supported caregivers of loved ones with brain-altering illnesses.

With OMS, Gord had served in the role of pastor to returning missionaries on home assignment and had led an effective and tender ministry. He had also recruited individuals and families, working with them as they prepared for service in their chosen country. He had given leadership to the Canadian office staff and worked well with the organization's board of directors.

Now all this work was a blur to him. We had many pictures from our time in these countries and the wonderful people we'd met along the way, but they meant less and less to Gord. It was very sad!

Eventually, he began to forget about me as well. Unfortunately, anger became an issue, too. He had difficulty controlling his emotions.

During a morning in October 2011, he lost control of his anger and I had to remove myself from him. This led to the lowest ebb of my life. My business was in the process of closing and I was fearful of randomly meeting Gord when I was out and about. His family soon moved him to a senior's apartment in London.

In 2012, I moved north back to the Minden area with my daughter Donna-Lee. This was not an easy decision, but I felt it was the next step in my recovery.

By 2013, Gord had divorced me. It took a long time to deal with the shock of our situation. Never in my life had I envisioned being a divorced woman, but I was thankful for my children and siblings who supported me no matter what. My seven grandchildren, ranging in age from two to sixteen, were sweet diversions for me. Despite the grey place in which I found myself, there were always blessings to turn to.

Within a year of our separation, I was diagnosed with coronary artery disease, which brought about the need for two stent implants in my heart. One of my doctors felt that I was suffering from broken heart syndrome and treated me accordingly.

Donna-Lee and I settled into sharing a home together. Angina plagued me and we paid many visits to the cardiologist before the medications began to work, providing more comfort. We had to take several trips to the emergency room for intervention to prevent a heart attack.

During these years, Donna-Lee and I had lots of good times, though, offering hospitality in our home, going out on day trips, and visiting family and friends. I felt at home in the Minden church where I had so many memories. This was comforting.

We eventually moved to Muskoka in 2015 to be of help to my youngest son Dean and his wife and their three children. Their marriage came to an unexpected and abrupt end within a short time, though, and Dean began sharing a home with us. His concern for his children was always on his mind. Within several weeks, the children began visiting for weekends and holidays. These visits were precious, although often rather stressful for this ole heart ticking inside my chest.

We rented a great home in the village of Novar, just north of Huntsville. Donna-Lee occupied the basement apartment, I took the studio apartment above the double garage, and Dean and his children settled into the four bedrooms on the second floor. The main part of the house included a large eat-in kitchen and a spacious living room. Although we all had access to the main part of the house, we often took our evening meals in my cozy cabin. It was the coolest apartment I've ever had!

We held our annual Christmas open house and New Year's Eve gatherings in that home, along with many celebrations with family and friends. The wrap-around veranda was a favourite spot for visiting over coffee and lemonade. For Halloween, the kids in the neighbourhood knew they could come to our well-lit veranda for treats. I had always wanted a house with a veranda and now I had it—at least, for a period of three years.

I had a rapport with my grandchildren, but I lacked the energy to be as active as I would have liked. Donna-Lee and I helped with a weekly kids club in our town, which was very rewarding. The COVID-19 pandemic, however, offered no favours in the department of the meaningful church fellowship I had known for six decades. We all struggled through these years, as so many others did. Even through the murky muddle in which I found my personal life, however, I sensed the closeness of God. His comfort has been real.

Donna-Lee has always determined to make the best of anything. During the eleven years we shared a home, we spent many warm summer mornings sharing laughs and reflective chats over coffee on the deck, and in the winter we could huddle around the fireplace with cups of tea. We were good companions.

She is a speaker, soloist, writer, and retreat organizer and pursued these interests as often as she could. Over the years, she's built an exceptional ministry, especially with children and women.

At the age of twenty, she was diagnosed with a benign brain tumour. It would have been risky to remove the tumour through surgery, because of its location, and so she was advised by surgeons to try to live with the symptoms. Those symptoms have caused issues throughout her adult life, holding her back from so many endeavours of which she is capable. There are many desires on her bucket list she has not yet been able to attempt. She has amazingly carried on, however, sensing God's strength in her weakness.

THIRTEEN
2020

With 2020 approaching, I couldn't help but think the number had a nice ring to it. As is my practice every December, I wondered what the next year might bring. Who could have known that 2020 would surely be a year to go down in history?

My family was planning a celebration for my seventy-fifth birthday in January. We were also going to celebrate the twenty-fifth anniversary of the miracle on Worchester Avenue.

The day before the celebration, a wicked freezing rainstorm hit, so it was cancelled. We rescheduled for May when one of my granddaughters would be returning from her semester of studies in Ireland.

Of course, that date never materialized due to the COVID-19 scare. Masks, paranoia, and isolation seemed to take over a large percentage of people's thinking for the next two years.

Going into the summer, we faced another crisis with Dean's family and he had the care of his two youngest children for several weeks. This occurred during a time when we were packing our household to move closer to Dean's work.

However, our anticipated new landlady suffered a fatal heart attack just before she could take possession of the house that she had intended to be our home. We scrambled to find a new rental since we had already given our notice in Novar.

Like so many other areas of Ontario, rentals in Muskoka were scarce. The Willows, who had been friends for several years, arranged for us to rent their home. We moved there in mid-October. Although we weren't any closer to Dean's work, we were ever so thankful to have a roof over our heads and ample room for all.

That home holds lots of good memories for us. We lived there for most of the following three years. The home had gorgeous wood beams and a log-house design, fulfilling my long desire to live in a log home someday.

Prior to moving into that home, I tripped over a box on September 1, taking an interesting tumble. I passed out at some point, and when I came to I was flat on my back, facing the opposite direction. I'm sure it would have made for a good laugh on home video, had someone been there to film it.

Fourteen hours in the ER determined that I had sustained soft tissue injuries on my left side, to the lower leg, knee, pelvis, and hand. I'd also suffered three whacks to the head. The attending physician couldn't believe a woman "of my age" could escape broken bones after that kind of fall!

The very colourful bruise to my leg began seeping five weeks later, leaving an open wound the size of a toonie. It took eight months to heal.

This slowed me down a bit while trying to do my part with unpacking and settling into a new home.

We finished the year by celebrating Christmas around a twelve-foot tree in our country kitchen with its high ceiling. With COVID still prevalent, limiting our regular gatherings, Donna-Lee decided to run a contest for people to guess the number of balls on this giant tree. Pictures were posted online and the guessing began. The prize was a dinner in our home, when allowed, or a gift card in the event that the winner was far away.

The contest was enjoyed by hundreds of people online, resulting in an adult finalist and a child finalist. It turned out there were 351 balls.

Several locals popped in for a few moments just to have a peak at the tree. Like so many families during COVID, we made our own fun.

FOURTEEN
Family Challenges

With the coming of the new year of 2021, Donna-Lee wasn't feeling well. She was given a diagnosis of congestive heart failure in March. Several visits to specialists occupied our time over the next six months. Tests were performed and new medications introduced, but still her health continued to deteriorate. This was a challenging time.

In August, I heard that Gord had passed following a few days in hospital. Our marriage had been broken for a decade, but I grieved the loss all over again.

On September 22, Donna-Lee was admitted to the hospital with necrotizing fasciitis, also known as flesh-eating disease. This began her extended ten-month hospital stay at the age of fifty-four. A new medication for blood sugar issues had been introduced just three weeks prior, and it was determined that this medication had caused the infection from the inside-out as a very rare side effect. How incredibly unfair that was for her, who already had such a physical struggle.

Surgery took place immediately, followed by five debridement surgeries over the next couple of weeks to remove destroyed or unhealthy tissues. She was eventually left with two gaping wounds the size of grapefruits.

On the third day of her twenty-one days in the ICU, she was crying in pain. She looked up at me as I stood by her bed and told me, "Just take the pain away."

I had a flashback of her first migraine at the age of five. She had looked up at me then as well, so many years ago, with the same sweet face, only smaller, and said the same thing.

Tears stung my cheeks again, feeling helpless.

She was already on very strong pain medications and strong antibiotics by IV. Her condition was life-threatening. We discussed palliative care as well as hospice. She was close to death several times, yet her body fought on.

Dean's two youngest children, James and Hannah, were allowed to visit Donna-Lee while she was still in the ICU. This was comforting and therapeutic for her, although she couldn't respond as she would have liked to respond. It was also quite an experience for the children to see her looking so fragile and pale, with tubes attached to her body. They had lost their maternal grandfather not long ago as he'd entered hospital for surgery, and then a complication had taken his life. It was important for them to know that the same outcome didn't necessarily happen to everyone who went to the hospital for surgery.

The children responded quite differently. One wanted to get as close as possible to their aunty and the other hung back. We respected both reactions.

This visit to the ICU provided meaningful conversations for the two grandchildren in the days to come, as they endeavoured to grasp an understanding of this part of life. They were later allowed to visit their aunt when she was able to be hoisted into a recliner on wheels and moved to the nearby chapel for a short visit. This, too, was good for everyone.

The church provided several meals for Dean and me, which was very much appreciated. With each visit to the hospital, I felt emotionally and physically drained, never knowing what next to expect. Prayers for Donna-Lee's comfort, healing, and recovery continued by hundreds of people. Prayers for my sustaining strength comforted me. Dean was my onsite rock.

Dwight and Donna faithfully visited Donna-Lee when she was in the Muskoka hospital. Their presence was very supportive for Dean and me as well. I so appreciated their love and concern.

Debra-Kaye and Andrew visited when they could make the trip north, as well as their Aunt Ruth from Minden.

My sister Joy and our brother Keith and his wife Bernice visited one September day as I took a lunch break from the hospital. That certainly brought me comfort that day. I cherished all these visits.

After two and a half months, Donna-Lee was transferred to a hospital in Ottawa for more effective wound care and treatment. One of her Bible college friends was able to visit her there before the next round of COVID restrictions prevented visitors again.

This was an exceptionally lonely time for Donna-Lee, seeing only hospital staff for months. The doctors and nurses recognized the adverse effects of the ongoing isolation on their patients while recovering from major life-threatening wounds. Most of the staff tried their best to provide encouragement, especially over the lonely Christmas season.

Talking to Donna-Lee over video chat helped us. Her face beamed to watch James and Hannah open their Christmas gifts and hear their cheers of joy. She often play games with them over the chat. Hangman, I Spy, anything with which they could include their aunty while moving about our home.

The first while in Ottawa was rough. In fact, her doctor later said that he had been losing her those first two weeks. But she eventually stabilized and slowly showed signs of progress in her recovery. Some days she was hoisted out of bed into a reclining chair. This was a painful procedure, though, and often she wasn't well enough to be moved.

After three and a half months in that hospital, her wounds were finally classified as healthy and the long process of further healing could get underway. The open holes still required dressing every other day, but she could be flown back to the Muskoka hospital.

Following another month, she was moved to a rehab unit in another Muskoka hospital where she stayed for three months. She had basically been bedridden for the previous six months and lost the ability to walk. The name of the game was learning how to transfer in and out of a wheelchair by herself.

Visitors were allowed during that time. I visited most days and Dean frequently dropped in before or after work. Dwight and Donna came regularly, Debra-Kaye and Andrew when they could, and her Aunt Ruth and Uncle Everett a few times. Eleanor, too, dropped in often, as well as Donna-Lee's pastor. Other good friends visited from near and far, including Val, Don, and Trudie. This was good therapy for her mind and soul.

As time moved along, she gained the ability to wheel herself outside into the fresh air for visits on an onsite patio. Besides this, she was so desperately weary of hospital meals that she looked forward to the food and snacks people brought in. We often had picnics on this patio.

James and Hannah weren't allowed inside the unit, but Dean would bring them to visit out on the patio as well.

This was very therapeutic. Donna-Lee appeared to be emerging from the dark place and small world she had been trapped in for so many months. She was able to glimpse the light ahead.

Donna-Lee was discharged in July 2022, a few days before her fifty-fifth birthday. A group of good friends helped by throwing her an ice cream social. She called it her Freedom 55 celebration. She was indeed pleased to be free of the hospital.

She came home with the use of a rented wheelchair and I became her full-time caregiver. I was pleased to be well enough to help her through the transition. She still had issues to work through and medications for a variety of conditions. An occupational therapist was instrumental in ordering everything she'd need. There was a shortage of personal support workers in the area, though, and physiotherapy didn't start until many months later.

Five months passed, by which time I wasn't well myself and had to make a trip to the hospital by ambulance. The diagnosis: double pneumonia with multifocal areas of infection, complicated by exhaustion. I remember feeling so very ill.

A three-day blizzard hit most of Ontario during the holidays, dropping four feet of snow outside my bedroom window. All this happened without my knowledge, because I slept through Christmas. I'm told that I apparently sat up on the sofa at some point for the gift-opening, but I don't remember it. I obviously did open gifts, because they were placed in my room to discover when I was more aware.

The new year came and went, and I recovered enough to enjoy a visit from Debra-Kaye and her girls for a weekend in mid-January. A few friends dropped in later for my birthday. I also have a vague memory of Mark visiting, the current executive director of the OMS office.

During the first few weeks of this illness, I had a recurring dream about drifting in outer space and fighting something. I know not what. I remember waking and asking God what it was all about before falling asleep again, only to return to the dream. I believe I was fighting for my life.

I was weak as a newborn pup and could no longer care for myself properly, let alone care for Donna-Lee. This was another challenging time, but friends from her church came to help as much as possible. My own recovery moved at a snail's pace.

A friend of mine from OMS, Alice Huff, told me about her own slow recovery from an illness.

"God isn't interested in rush jobs," she said. "Seldom does He do things in quite the way I'd plan, but His timing is perfect. He lovingly allows the delays that build in His children patience and perseverance."

This is so true. I would also add that it was another good exercise in character building.

Our home was designed with an inviting little interior balcony off the upstairs apartment dining room. It overlooked the landing on the beautiful set of stairs that led down to the main entrance just outside Donna-Lee's apartment. Those stairs separated she from me, me from her. She couldn't come up the stairs, and while I could make my way down, it was most difficult to push my weakened body back up. However, we could visit when I came to the balcony and she arrived at the main entrance below. We shared morning coffee and lunch breaks this way on our better days. It was the best we could do.

By Easter, I went to Strathroy with Debra-Kaye and Andrew to continue recovering. Uncontrolled high blood pressure plagued me for most of 2023 and I was pleased when my former family doctor, as well as an internist, took me back as a patient during these post-COVID years when doctors were hard to come by.

From December 2022 through April 2023, I was too tired to cry, even during stressful events that in the past would have caused the shedding of tears. Since May, it seems that my tear ducts are too close to the surface. Tears flow easily and my emotions are rather unpredictable at times. The return of my tears, though, brings hope for more recovery to come.

During the challenges of these years, one ray of sunshine in my life has been my ability to support a young missionary family serving in Peru. The Coopers have three sons. They remind me of my brother Morley, his wife Darlene, and their three sons as they established their ministry in Ecuador. I have the privilege to partner with the Coopers in their ministry in building relationships, doing life together with the Peruvians, and sharing the gospel along the way.

FIFTEEN
Aftermath

At the time of this writing in December 2023, I am waiting for my name to top the waitlist for an apartment in a retirement community in Strathroy. I am both retired and recovered, although I know God may have something else in mind for the rest of this journey. I leave that with Him.

I am thankful to have had the time and to concentrate sufficiently on writing this autobiography based on material I collected throughout the years, including presentations and documents I filed away for when the day came for this journey would be written, whether by myself or someone else.

On the day of the miracle on Worchester Avenue—February 20, 1995—God asked if I would share with others what He was doing in my life. This question has spurred me on these last thirty years to share whenever, however, and wherever I have found myself to be. I have felt compelled to do so.

I must thank Debra-Kaye and Andrew for sharing their home throughout my lengthy recovery and looking after me when required. They have provided a pleasant room, with my computer sitting on my Grandpa Miller's charming desk, which he made in the early 1900s. I remember him sitting at this desk while looking after the farm finances. There is a window before me with a view of their well-groomed back yard, butting a conservation area. Squirrels, chipmunks, rabbits, deer, and a variety of beautiful birds often come into view. They are very entertaining.

During the most stressful seasons of Donna-Lee's hospitalization, I couldn't concentrate enough to read my Bible. One day as I sat at my desk—motionless, numb, staring at the wall—I noticed the calendar from OMS Canada. Their calendars always have a scripture for each month. I determined to read the monthly verse over and over until I had it memorized. For several months, these verses became my only meaningful contact with the Bible.

A few friends had taken up the mantle to visit me during those months while I was still in Muskoka. They kept in touch by phone, brought in prepared meals and thoughtful items for us, cleaned our apartment, and drove me to medical appointments. Their help and prayer support enabled me to weave my way through those months of early recovery.

Dean was my onsite rock. He is so much like his dad. He is quiet and has faith in God and a good work ethic. He also requires a good night's sleep. I could always count on him to return home from work to share the evening meal with me, buying groceries and doing errands as required.

Since I have relocated to Strathroy, Dean and Donna-Lee continue to share a home. Their recent move to Bala, following a couple stressful months, finally brought them closer to Dean's work. James and Hannah continue to come on weekends and holidays. Donna-Lee's desire to live in view of a lake has been fulfilled, for they all enjoy a beautiful view of Lake Muskoka. They make a good family, supporting and helping one another even when the days are rough.

Donna-Lee continues to make progress in her recovery, and she now has the help of community support services. Dean deserves brownie points for caring for his sister. I am proud of the way his children also adjusted to their aunt's life in a wheelchair. They are her helpers indeed. James and Hannah love their Aunty Donna-Lee. She loves them dearly and spoils them royally.

CONCLUSION
A Lifetime

One fine Saturday afternoon in the late spring of 1960, Mom made a profound comment. A hot pot of tea and freshly baked cookies rested on the kitchen table.

"When your dad and I were married, we were so much in love," she said. "We thought we could turn the world upside-down, get involved with various people, touch their lives, and make a difference. As time moved on, we got busy just making a life for our family. We decided that we wouldn't be turning the world upside-down, but maybe your generation would make that difference in people's lives, and your children will, and their children."

This solemn remark was rather out of character for Mom. I listened and filed it away in the recesses of my brain, retrieving her words periodically over the sixty-five years to follow.

We then paused the conversation, poured our tea, and changed the subject. Mom and I never did return to that line of comment.

For context, my parents were married in 1940. World War II was underway and Dad's health had prevented him from being enlisted. When the war ended in September 1945, they had three children. Like so many Canadian families, they worked hard in those post-war years to make a living.

I believe my parents truly made a difference for many people, Mom in her quiet and gentle way through her ninety years on this earth and Dad through his businesses. Both had a superb work ethic, cared for others, and taught their children the value of work and demonstrating compassion to those who crossed their paths. They made a good life for me and my siblings and we loved them dearly. Of all the parents in the world, we were truly grateful they were ours.

My dad's father, Walter Johnson, had immigrated to Canada from Wales at the turn of the twentieth century. He had married an Algonquin lady who lived in the area, and they settled in a log house south of Hawk Lake Road in Haliburton County. They were blessed with six children.

My dad, Doward, was the fourth child in his family, born in 1912. When their mother passed away, he was six. His older sister Ida was twelve, Tracy was ten, and Norman was eight. The second youngest, Elvin, was four. He was taken in by a Christian family nearby. As for the youngest, two-year-old Rose, she was subsequently adopted by a family in a different area. Tracy had wanted to keep in touch with the family Rose ended up with, but that turned out not to be possible.

Those decisions must have been tough, and Aunt Ida looked after the household after that.

Grandpa Johnson and Uncle Norman died from pneumonia in 1926. Since my dad was fourteen by that time, having finished Grade Six, he was considered old enough to go to work. He moved to a farm near Minden and started his career.

In his early twenties, he was diagnosed with grand mal seizures and taken to a hospital in Guelph for treatment. When well enough, he worked at a nearby farm, reporting back at the hospital for regular treatments and checkups. The shock treatments used in that era to treat epilepsy were effective, but they wiped out his memory of life before the age of twenty.

In time, he made his way back to Haliburton County and met his bride-to-be. Dad and Mom were married in 1940 and the rest is history. Dad's seizures never returned, although he was left with night sweats that plagued him for the rest of his life.

About thirty years after Grampa Johnson died, my Uncle Tracy began searching for his sister Rose. He followed many leads and searched for more than a decade. Eventually she was found living in central Ontario.

Aunt Rose had driven through Haliburton County often without having any idea she had siblings there. We all rejoiced when she was found. Aunt Rose attended our wedding in 1966. Her presence made the day extra special for the entire Johnson family.

Into my adult years, I became close to Uncle Elvin and Aunt Ruby and their three sons. After my dad passed away, Uncle Elvin filled in nicely. He was like a dad to me and I loved them dearly.

Uncle Elvin was dedicated to bettering his community, volunteering as a firefighter. His lobbying directly resulted in the building of a fire hall and community centre. He always pushed to keep portage and parkland open so the public could enjoy the area's natural beauty. He also served on council for many years.

He developed a park in the Algonquin Highlands which was named the Elvin Johnson Park in 1998 when he was named citizen of the year. The park continues to be used by many locals and tourists and is well cared for.

He and Aunt Ruby stretched their horizons many ways during their married years, including making trips to Ecuador to help his nephew, my brother Morley, with community work. He also took a brush in hand and began painting sceneries in his eightieth year. Even though his life is over, his name lives on. Aunt Ruby passed in 2009. I miss them both.

My mom's family was a mix of German and Scottish descent. Grandpa Miller was a farmer. They spent their married life on the property where he was born, near Minden. He was a quiet man until he suffered a fatal heart attack after working a field not far from home. My grandmother lived for another twenty-nine years and died a few days after a debilitating stroke. She had just celebrated her eighty-seventh birthday. I dearly miss her!

My mom passed in October 2010, six weeks before her ninetieth birthday. At the age of eighty-seven, she was diagnosed with congestive heart failure. She then had to take medications daily for the first time in her life. She still lived at home, caring for most of the work although my brother and sister were close by to help as needed.

In the summer of 2010, we celebrated her upcoming birthday. This was a time of year when all of her children and most of her grandchildren and great-grandchildren could attend. She was very happy to see everyone together, although somewhat puzzled as to why we would celebrate her birthday so early. She didn't like to think of herself as ninety yet, but there was her family celebrating it anyway. We had a delicious picnic in her own backyard, with everyone bringing their specialities for the occasion. It was a lovely afternoon. I miss her every day.

I wish to include some information on those children, grandchildren, and great-grandchildren to whom my mother alluded all those years ago when she expressed the desire for her descendants to make more of a difference in their lives.

My sister Joy was one of five high school girls who wrote a book for the Haliburton County centennial called *Remembering When*. They visited many seniors in the county, interviewing and recording their memories. The following summer, this information was compiled into a book.

Joy has always been interested in researching alternative health helps, not only for herself but for others. Her work in a health store for many years touched numerous people during their times of vulnerability. She is a wonderful seamstress and creative in designing clothes, quilts, stuffed toys. She has used her loom to make many beautiful items.

She was part of the parenting team for an incredible young fellow named Jordan, who has become a professor in his own right.

Joy has long struggled with muscular sclerosis, and her goal has been to be the healthiest MS patient in the universe. She and her husband Steve live on a property near Minden where she grows and prepares much of her food. Her perseverance is an encouragement and inspiration to many. I'm proud to call her my sister!

Keith has touched many lives through his businesses. He also had lots of people contact while racing sleds through the Ontario circuit. He still participates in gun-range activities with locals and visitors from afar. He operated a go-kart track and then a hair salon for many years.

He ended his career driving big rig haulers across Canada and the United States and now spends his time reading and researching his many interests. Keith and his wife Bernice have raised two fine sons, Blaine and Blair.

When Keith celebrated his eightieth birthday, I asked him if he finally felt his age, and his response was that he felt fifty. More power to him! He has been the healthy one in our family: tall, handsome and never looking his age.

Morley had many opportunities to touch people's lives with his work in Ecuador for twenty-five years. He, too, was a people person. Morley and Darlene had three sons born to them while in Ecuador: Brian, Philip and Tim.

When I visited Ecuador after both Morley and Murray had passed, Darlene introduced me to many of their good Ecuadorian friends. They included phoneline workers, farmers, shopkeepers, neighbours, government officials, ditchdiggers, teachers, pastors, engineers, army officers, and doctors. His life attracted like-minded people of faith as well as those who didn't share his beliefs.

On September 25, 2023, I took note that it would have been my parents' eighty-third wedding anniversary. All these years later, one of their great-granddaughters made her decision to further her education while continuing to serve as a nurse. Another great-granddaughter began her first day as a teacher, following six years of study in university. The sky is the limit for these young adults and their cousins as they move along in today's workforce.

One of my parents' grandsons recently reached his goal in the aviation world by becoming an instructor and line check pilot for United Airlines, a company he has been with for sixteen years. He has flown 1,800 hours in the Boeing 757 and 767 and 9,100 hours in the Boing 737, which he currently flies. As the captain, he also flies with new first officers and captains until they have flown the required flight time and show the necessary proficiency to work without supervision.

All of my parents' many family members continue to do their part, touching lives as teachers, business managers, office workers, writers, speakers, early childhood educators, hunting guides, township office staff, bus drivers, road workers, heavy equipment operators, domestic engineers, seamstresses, firefighters, salesmen, carpenters, truckers, nurses, and pilots, not unlike so many families in this twenty-first century.

In 2023, I watched a European travel show hosted by Rick Steves focused on Christmas. It did my heart good to see so many beautiful scenes from England, Norway, France, Germany, Austria, Italy, and Switzerland. There were scenes of countryside, beautifully decorated town squares, shops and outdoor markets, and cookies being baked. The show depicted traditional Christmas meals being prepared in home kitchens, trees being decorated, and candlelight services being held in churches and on streets. The scenes included traditional gift-making and gift-giving and visits to many homes with candles, bows, greenery everywhere. Many traditional Christmas choirs sang carols of the birth of Jesus.

As I reflected on my own life of nearly eighty years, this program reminded me of God's goodness in giving me the desires of my heart to travel the world. He knew my strengths and weaknesses and my desire to make my life count for His glory in so many ways.

There is a familiar poem, "Footprints in the Sand" by Margaret Fisher Powers, that depicts the Lord walking alongside a man during his lifetime. The picture often accompanying the poem shows two sets of footprints on a beautiful sandy beach. However, at times we see only one set of footprints. The man recalls these are the times when he was at his lowest ebb, desperately in need of the Lord's help and comfort. Assuming the single set of footprints are his own, the man questions the Lord, "Why did you abandon me?" The Lord lovingly tells him that these were the occasions when He carried him.

Our Lord carries us! It's important to be able to identify this awesome fact. Life often includes seasons that are rough, challenging, and seemingly out of our control. There are also times when life is good. Bask in those good times. Everyone knows that life can change at a moment's notice. We are here for a purpose, living in the land God has created, no matter how smooth or messy it is. As a believer we can rest assured that the Lord has been, is, and will be carrying us because He is faithful! The least we can do is be faithful to our calling.

Be blessed.

Dwight and Donna in 1998.

PJ's grandchildren in 2007.
Front: Luke, Caitlin, and Alyssa. Back: Kyla and Madison.

PJ with her daughter Donna-Lee and son Dean, along with grandchildren Hannah and James in 2019.

Debra-Kaye and Andrew in 2020.

PJ in 2024.